Our world is amazing, and Michael Guillen is one of the best communicators of science out there. Michael's fascinating knowledge of the natural world and our place in the universe are perfectly complemented by the devotional insights he shares from Scripture. This book will leave you in awe and wonder at the Maker whose handiwork is displayed all around us, and who chose to enter his creation to give himself for us.

JUSTIN BRIERLEY, author of *The Surprising Rebirth of Belief in God* and former host of the *Unbelievable?* podcast

"I'm inviting you to embark on a life-changing adventure designed to rescue you from the monotony and smallness of your everyday life." With those words, scientist Michael Guillen helps us consider both Scripture and science as means for spiritual growth. *Let Creation Speak!* is set up as a series of one hundred short, stand-alone essays. Michael guides us to consider grains of sand on the beach, South Pacific volcanoes, and Bolivia's giant water lily, as well as the stars in the sky (he trained at Cornell in physics, mathematics, and astronomy, after all), and of course the Bible. Through these essays, we see more closely the goodness of God's care for us as Creator and Redeemer. As he writes about this book, "It's an invitation for you to open your mind to the possibility that all of it—from the immortal jellyfish and wandering albatross to the jewel wasp and giant tubeworm—is not merely an accident, but the intentional creation of a being that himself is beyond comprehension." This is a beautiful and edifying journey. I commend you to take it with an entirely able and fascinating guide, Michael Guillen.

GREG COOTSONA, codirector of Science for the Church and author of *Mere Science and Christian Faith: Bridging the Divide with Emerging Adults*

"The heavens proclaim the glory of God," says Psalm 19:1. And we can see God's "eternal power and divine nature" through what he has made, says Romans 1:20. But what does *science* say? In *Let Creation Speak!*, Dr. Michael Guillen unpacks an amazing array of scientific examples, which together compose a compelling news flash: *Science and Scripture are friends! They point to the same realities!* I'm confident you'll find these readings both fascinating and fun—and spiritually fulfilling as well.

MARK MITTELBERG, executive director of the Lee Strobel Center for Evangelism and Applied Apologetics at Colorado Christian University (StrobelCenter.com), and author of *Confident Faith* and *The Questions Christians Hope No One Will Ask (With Answers)*

Let Creation Speak!

Let Creation Speak

!

100 INVITATIONS TO AWE AND WONDER

Michael Guillen, PhD

FORMER ABC NEWS SCIENCE EDITOR

Author of the #1 Amazon Bestseller *Believing Is Seeing*

TYNDALE
REFRESH

Think Well. Live Well. Be Well.

Visit Tyndale online at tyndale.com.

Visit Tyndale Refresh online at tyndalerefresh.com.

Tyndale, Tyndale's quill logo, *Tyndale Refresh*, and the Tyndale Refresh logo are registered trademarks of Tyndale House Ministries. Tyndale Refresh is a nonfiction imprint of Tyndale House Publishers, Carol Stream, Illinois.

Let Creation Speak!: 100 Invitations to Awe and Wonder

Designed by Dean H. Renninger

The author is represented by Ambassador Literary, Nashville, TN.

For information about special discounts for bulk purchases, please contact Tyndale House Publishers at csresponse@tyndale.com, or call 1-855-277-9400.

ISBN 987-1-4964-7355-4

Printed in the United States of America

29	28	27	26	25	24	23
7	6	5	4	3	2	1

For the Artist of creation,

whom I love with all my heart, soul, mind, and strength.

Soli Deo Gloria!

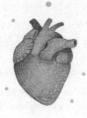

Contents

Introduction

Is the universe more than just a cosmic accident? Is there more to life than your daily grind? Is it possible you actually have a divine purpose?

Yes. Yes. Yes.

Wherever you are in life—and whether you're a Christian, like me, or an Atheist, like I used to be, or something else—this book is an invitation. I'm inviting you to open your eyes and ears to the myriad wonders all around you—and even inside you.

Accept my invitation and you will be more than amazed by this book's doses of sheer wonder—you will be radically transformed.

Yes, *transformed.*

According to the Bible, the only way to become a genuinely new person—the only way to break free from your small worldview and dull routine—is by seeing and thinking about the universe in a whole new way:

> *Let God transform you into a new person by changing the way you think. Then you will learn to know God's will for you, which is good and pleasing and perfect.*[1]

Whether you are young or old, I'm inviting you to embark on a life-changing adventure designed to rescue you from the monotony and smallness of your everyday life. To *change* you, profoundly and permanently. To help you find and embrace the radiant, resilient, relevant person you were created to be.

Don't miss this opportunity. Starting right here and now, *let God and his creation speak . . . directly to you!*

Unimaginable

There was a time when we believed the universe was finite in size. Not anymore. Today, based on what we've learned using powerful telescopes, spacecraft, and other clever devices, we realize the size of the universe is truly incomprehensible.

For starters, the sun is roughly 1.3 million times bigger than Earth. Of the solar system's total mass, 99.8 percent of it belongs to the sun, only 0.2 percent belongs to all the planets, moons, and asteroids combined.

Our solar system is located within the Milky Way galaxy, which contains roughly 200 billion stars, our beloved, life-sustaining sun being just one of them and of average size. The Milky Way itself is also of average size, yet it takes a beam of light 120,000 years to cross it; a commercial jetliner would take 150 *billion* years.

According to our best estimates, the observable universe contains roughly 200 billion galaxies, many of them far bigger than our Milky Way. Assuming each galaxy contains at least 200 billion stars, it means the observable universe contains more than forty billion trillion (40,000,000,000,000,000,000,000) stars—and even more planets than that.

And that's just the *observable* cosmos.

We now know that outside the observable cosmos—past the asteroids, moons, planets, stars, and galaxies of this world; past its invisible dark energy and dark matter; past what astronomers call the *cosmic horizon*—is a universe that is and always will be hidden from us, an unobservable world whose size and nature is, and always will be, *beyond* human comprehension.

REFLECTION

There are many people who use the unimaginable size of the universe to diminish our own significance. They claim that since our solar system is a mere speck in the great scheme of things—and we humans are even tinier whits on that mere speck—we aren't important at all.

But there's another way of seeing things.

There are more than 40 billion trillion stars in the observable universe—many of them far bigger and flashier than our own mediocre sun; and there are even more planets than that in the observable universe. But despite centuries of searching and searching, we have found *zero* planets with any kind of life, let alone human life.

For now, then, far from being insignificant, our seemingly lowly sun and planet are *beyond significant*. So next time you look up and marvel at the unimaginable size of the observable cosmos—and the even more unimaginable world beyond the cosmic horizon—stop and marvel at the one who's doing the marveling.

Stop and marvel at *yourself*, and at the ineffable God who created you—and the unimaginable universe you call home.

THE CREATOR SPEAKS

The heavens proclaim the glory of God.
 The skies display his craftsmanship.
Day after day they continue to speak;
 night after night they make him known.
They speak without a sound or word;
 their voice is never heard.
Yet their message has gone throughout the earth,
 and their words to all the world.

PSALM 19:1-4

A Brand-New You

In 1883, a German biologist exploring the Mediterranean Sea discovered a tiny jellyfish he named *Turritopsis dohrnii*. Roughly as big as the tip of your little finger—about 4.5 mm (3/16") across—it has a transparent, bell-shaped body, a bright red stomach, and scores of tiny, translucent white tentacles. It loves eating plankton and fish eggs.

How long does it live? That's the fascinating part. Scientists have discovered that *T. dohrnii* has the ability to live forever!

A typical, garden-variety jellyfish goes through five stages of growth. Starting from a fertilized egg, it morphs into a larva, then a polyp, then a baby jellyfish (called an ephyra), and finally into an adult jellyfish (called a medusa). A medusa usually dies right after reproducing.

But not *T. dohrnii*. Amazingly, it can revert to the polyp stage at will. Whenever it is at risk of dying, this unique creature instantly sinks to the bottom of the ocean and transforms into a brand-new polyp—a brand-new self. From there, it once again goes through the various stages of growth and becomes a born-again medusa.

This process of being "born again" is a mystery to science, but it goes by the name of *transdifferentiation*. As far as scientists can tell, *T. dohrnii* can stay alive this way indefinitely. For that reason, it's called the immortal jellyfish.

REFLECTION

Are you tired of being *you*? Through spiritual transdifferentiation, and the unlimited power of the Holy Spirit, God can remake you from the inside out and ensure that when your old self dies, your new self will live forever.

To get started, just hit the reset button, like the immortal jellyfish. Simply admit out loud your dissatisfaction with yourself and ask for

God's help. He will do the rest. Let your old, tired, dying life sink to the bottom of the abyss, then rise up and be reborn!

THE CREATOR SPEAKS

Anyone who belongs to Christ has become a new person.
The old life is gone; a new life has begun!
2 CORINTHIANS 5:17

State of Being

Nobody wants to be touched, bitten, or stung by a toxic plant or animal. Nevertheless, in one of the great ironies of creation, there are dangerous plants and animals whose noxious chemical ingredients have the potential to become, or inspire, lifesaving drugs.

Scientists have already created scores of such medications. At this very minute, these miraculous meds are being used to successfully treat chronic pain and other serious afflictions, such as hypertension, diabetes, and heart failure.

Scientists estimate that tens of thousands more such unlikely wonder drugs await discovery or study. One of them comes from a snake called the black mamba (*Dendroaspis polylepis*)—the deadliest serpent in the world after the king cobra (*Ophiophagus hannah*).

Native to sub-Saharan Africa, black mambas can grow to be fourteen feet long. As one of the fastest snake species, the mamba can shoot forward at more than twelve miles per hour. Its bite delivers a neurotoxin that very quickly shuts down its victim's nervous system and brain function.

Yet, despite that danger, the black mamba's dreaded venom contains *mambalgins*, peptides that can relieve pain as effectively as morphine but *without any adverse side effects*. Mambalgins won't cause respiratory failure, are nonaddictive, and don't numb the body; they simply disable pain receptors.

You can understand, then, why scientists are so eagerly scouring the whole of creation for other such hidden gems—medicines of great beauty and value disguised as substances of enormous terror and revulsion.

REFLECTION

Life has a way of biting and stinging us with sudden misfortune and outright calamity. At first, we shake our fists at God, or at fate, for our situation, seeing absolutely no silver lining.

Yet, often as not, there are redeeming qualities—unlikely gemstones—hidden deep within the painful experience. It makes about as much sense as a deadly venom having lifesaving properties, but it's true—it's a *translogical* truth. (See also Invitations 29, 70, and 88.)

Many people who have suffered unspeakable hardship not only survived but also discovered an indescribable peace and even joy they never would have experienced otherwise. Adversity can bring unexpected and illogical blessings.

A successful nineteenth-century American lawyer named Horatio Spafford exemplifies this baffling, translogical truth. He lost his only son, a four-year-old, to scarlet fever; then he lost his entire real-estate fortune in the Great Chicago Fire of 1871; then he lost all four of his daughters, aged eighteen months to twelve years, in a cruise ship accident.

It was like being bitten by an entire nest of black mambas. Yet, despite it all—in fact, *because* of it all—Spafford was inspired to write the now-famous hymn "It Is Well with My Soul." It's an homage to a translogical truth that continues to help countless others around the world rise above their own devastations.

The Bible warns us point-blank to expect hardships; there's nothing we can do about it. But it also says this: We have control over how we *respond* to our disasters.

We can let them take us down. Or we can allow them to elevate us to an incomprehensible, translogical, joyful state of being.

THE CREATOR SPEAKS

When troubles of any kind come your way, consider it an opportunity for great joy. For you know that when your faith is tested, your endurance has a chance to grow. So let it grow, for when your endurance is fully developed, you will be perfect and complete, needing nothing.

JAMES 1:2-4

Resilience

When we dig into Earth's rocky layers, we dig into its past, as though we were in a time machine. By counting fossils as we go, we get a rough idea of how Earth's populations of plants and animals have waxed and waned over time.

By doing that, geologists have evidence that our planet has been rocked by no fewer than five mass extinctions. Five mysterious catastrophes that nearly wiped the slate clean.

First came the Ordovician mass extinction. It reportedly killed up to 85 percent of all life on Earth.

Second came the Devonian mass extinction. It reportedly killed up to 80 percent of all life on Earth.

Third came the Permian mass extinction. It reportedly killed a whopping 96 percent of all life on Earth—the worst of the bunch.

Fourth came the Triassic-Jurassic mass extinction. It reportedly killed more than half of all life on the planet.

Fifth came the K-T mass extinction. It reportedly killed nearly 75 percent of all life, including the mighty dinosaurs. For that reason, it's the most well-known of all mass extinctions.

Scientists don't know exactly what caused any of these calamitous events, but they have come up with possible culprits. They include impacts by comets or asteroids, widespread volcanic eruptions, deoxygenated oceans, and killer microbes.

Whatever the causes were, at least two things are crystal clear: (1) Mass extinctions are a normal fact of life on planet Earth, and (2) Earth's geology and climate can change on a dime, all on its own, for reasons we don't understand.

Remarkably, not only has Earth survived all five mass extinctions, it has *flourished*—ultimately producing the planet we cherish so much today.

REFLECTION

Have you ever personally experienced a mass extinction? A time when everything you cherished was wiped out? If so, the Bible offers you hope by chronicling the story of a godly man named Job.

In a short period of time, Job lost all his wealth: 7,000 sheep, 3,000 camels, 500 teams of oxen, 500 female donkeys; all his many servants; and all ten of his beloved children—seven sons and three daughters.

Then he himself was physically afflicted "with terrible boils from head to foot." This was so painful that he desperately sought relief by scraping "his skin with a piece of broken pottery as he sat among the ashes."[1]

Horrified by Job's ghastly fall from grace, his wife urged him to turn on God, shrieking: "Are you still trying to maintain your integrity? Curse God and die."[2]

But Job did no such thing. Instead he said: "You talk like a foolish woman. . . . The Lord gave me what I had, and the Lord has taken it away. Praise the name of the Lord!"[3]

Next, Job's three best friends—Eliphaz, Bildad, and Zophar—accused him of *deserving* his sudden misfortune. But Job insisted he was blameless.

Finally, God himself got on Job's case, calling him out for his hubris. For Job, that was the last straw; he broke down and pleaded for forgiveness, which God granted.

More than that, God healed Job, as a reward for his unshakable faith. After that, Job had ten more children and ended up with twice as many sheep, camels, oxen, and donkeys as before.

THE CREATOR SPEAKS

You have allowed me to suffer much hardship,
    but you will restore me to life again
    and lift me up from the depths of the earth.
You will restore me to even greater honor
    and comfort me once again.

PSALM 71:20-21

Truth Hurts

Horror movies often use tarantulas (family Theraphosidae) to scare us. But in truth, tarantulas aren't particularly dangerous—except, that is, for their hairy stomachs.

Tarantulas are hairy everywhere on their bodies, but only the stomach hairs—called *urticating* hairs—are dangerous. Unlike regular hairs, which are made of a protein called keratin, urticating hairs are tiny, barbed bristles made of a tough, plastic-like material called chitin.

When threatened, a tarantula will fling a cluster of these tiny spears at its enemy. These barbed bristles are very good at felling small prey and keeping away large predators.

We humans need to worry about the lances getting into our eyes or mouth. Like slender shards of glass or fine needles of fiberglass, they can cause serious irritation, or worse.

To protect themselves from such spear attacks, people who keep tarantulas wear long-sleeve shirts, gloves, and eye protection whenever they handle their spiders or clean out their cages.

In contrast to its dangerous stomach hairs, a tarantula's body hairs are entirely safe and quite remarkable.

Because tarantulas don't see very well (despite having eight eyes), and they don't have ears, they rely on their fine body hairs to get around. Incredibly, the delicate hairs, called trichobothria, sense tiny changes in air pressure caused by nearby obstacles, predators, or prey—for example, even something as subtle as the beating of a fly's wings.

REFLECTION

Think back to when you were in school: Hearing a teacher say you failed a test probably felt as awful as getting an eyeful of little tarantula stomach spears. Nothing hurts quite like the truth.

For that reason, the Bible commands you to speak the truth with *love*. Keep that in mind whenever you're in a position to correct someone.

At the same time, be sure not to make the opposite mistake of loving people without speaking the truth to them. If someone makes a mistake or behaves badly, genuine love requires a word of correction.

In short, truth without love and love without truth are equally hurtful and condemnable. Strive to relate to others in a way that's both encouraging and enlightening.

THE CREATOR SPEAKS

This is what you must do: Tell the truth to each other. Render verdicts in your courts that are just and that lead to peace.
ZECHARIAH 8:16

A Win/Win

Rhinoceroses (family Rhinocerotidae) sport mean-looking horns, grow up to six feet tall, and weigh as much as 7,500 pounds—heavier than most passenger cars. With all that going for them, you'd think they'd terrorize any animal that crossed their path; but they don't, for one simple reason: Rhinos are vegetarians.

Other aspects of a rhino's tough, outward persona are equally deceiving. For instance, their skin is thick and tough, like plate armor, but it's also surprisingly sensitive.

A rhino's tough hide sunburns easily, so during the day the poor beast is constantly, desperately looking for shade. That's why you so frequently see rhinos wallowing in the mud; it's a natural sunscreen.

Mud also helps protect against the legions of insects, parasites, and ticks that plague a rhino's sensitive skin. The only problem is, hot temperatures cause the mud on a rhino to harden and crack, creating openings that hungry insects immediately storm.

Thankfully, rhinos have yet another layer of protection: the yellow-billed oxpecker (*Buphagus africanus*), an African bird that rides on a rhino's back and feeds on the many ticks and other noxious insects attacking the rhino's skin. Because rhinos have very poor eyesight, they also depend on the oxpeckers to sound the alarm whenever danger is near.

The birds' piercing cries not only alert the rhinos, but also help scare away any would-be predators, even human poachers. In exchange for providing all these life-preserving services, the oxpeckers get free food and free rides over long distances.

It's a win/win situation scientists call a *symbiotic relationship*.

REFLECTION

Rhinos remind us that appearances can be deceiving. Someone with a slight, nonthreatening build might really be quite dangerous. A dangerous-looking, heavyweight pro boxer who destroys opponents in the ring might really be a gentle giant.

Most of us are both things—dangerously aggressive and wonderfully gentle. But the Bible commands us to be gentle always.

When someone behaves aggressively toward you, the Bible says to turn the other cheek. That doesn't mean tolerating abuse; it means not repaying evil with evil.

When someone is being cowed by some terrifying crisis, the Bible tells you not to take advantage of them. Instead, encourage them with prayers, your friendship, and whatever other practical help you can give.

The Bible explains and scientific research affirms that when you do that, you *yourself* are blessed, just as an oxpecker is rewarded for helping rhinoceroses. It's a deep, spiritual version of a symbiotic relationship.

THE CREATOR SPEAKS

> Share each other's burdens, and
> in this way obey the law of Christ.
> GALATIANS 6:2

The Gift
of Leadership

Walk among any sprawling community of trees and you'll see trunks, branches, and leaves. But to behold a forest's true nature, you must look beneath the soil.

When you do that, you'll quickly spot what Dr. Suzanne Simard, professor of forest ecology at the University of British Columbia, calls the Mother Trees. They're a forest's oldest and tallest members.

By virtue of having been born first and survived the longest, Mother Trees tower over their forest companions, basking in unshaded sunlight. That photosynthetic advantage means that Mother Trees typically produce more sugar, carbon, and nitrogen than they themselves need.

What happens to the excess nutrients? The Mother Trees distribute them to their fellow trees via a vast subterranean web of fungal fibers called a *mycorrhizal network*.

All of a forest's many root systems are part of a single mycorrhizal network, so every tree can partake of the Mother Trees' largesse. It's an extraordinary system of selflessness that is of particular importance to seedlings, which struggle to grow in the shade of their older, taller neighbors.

It's also of crucial importance during periods of drought and other extreme stress. At such times, the generosity of Mother Trees can spare an entire forest from otherwise certain debilitation and even death.

REFLECTION

Any community, business, household, or place of worship benefits enormously from people who generously and cheerfully contribute their time, talents, and treasure. But all too often, it's only a small number of such people who, like Mother Trees, do most of the heavy lifting.

These leaders are often born, not made. The Bible describes them as having the *gift* of leadership: Instinctively, they have a special knack for managing people and situations, especially during crises.

But leaders are also made. Often these special souls have been through hellish fires that left them with invaluable survival skills, empathy, and a deep spirit of generosity.

Because of these remarkable Mother Trees—leaders born and made—we're all better off. These benefactors are precious gifts from God, truly the mother of all Mother Trees.

THE CREATOR SPEAKS

Don't be selfish; don't try to impress others. Be humble, thinking of others as better than yourselves. Don't look out only for your own interests, but take an interest in others, too.
PHILIPPIANS 2:3-4

Creating Sparks

You, your clothes, and everything around you are made of atoms. Normally, each atom is electrically neutral: Its positively charged core cancels out its surrounding swarm of negatively charged electrons.

But when you rub together certain materials, you upset that delicate balance. The materials shed electrons, and suddenly sparks begin to fly.

In the 1930s, the Canadian and American prairies were plagued by a series of severe dust storms. Sand particles rubbing against air molecules created such an electrical imbalance that sparks flew everywhere, causing cars, machinery, and radios to short-circuit. When people shook hands, the sparks between them knocked both parties to the ground.

More recently, in 2005, an Australian named Frank Clewer went to a job interview wearing a woolen shirt and nylon jacket. Unbeknownst to him, the nylon started rubbing electrons off the wool, creating an electrical imbalance.

At first, all he heard was the *snap*, *crackle*, and *pop* of static electricity. But by the time he entered the building for his interview, the sparks were so intense they actually set fire to the carpeted floor.

The frantic business owners called the fire department and ordered a mass evacuation of the building. Once on the scene, first responders identified Mr. Clewer as the culprit and estimated that the sparks flying off his clothing would register at 40,000 volts![1]

REFLECTION

Inevitably, there are times when you meet someone who rubs you the wrong way—or whom you rub the wrong way. When that happens— *look out!*—sparks are likely to fly.

Sometimes the instant antagonism is easy to identify: A person's thoughtless remark or facial expression is enough to set you off. Other times it's harder to figure out, in which case we usually chalk it up to a clash of personalities.

Either way, the imbalance caused by the friction is enough to set fire not just to a carpet, but to an entire family, church, or workplace. And make no mistake, everyone knows that you and the other person are the culprits.

The only way to avoid such clashes is to watch carefully what you wear—your *attitude*, not your clothing.

Remember, it takes *two* dissimilar materials to create sparks. So whenever you meet people who rub you the wrong way, do your best not to respond by rubbing *them* the wrong way.

THE CREATOR SPEAKS

A gentle answer deflects anger,
    but harsh words make tempers flare.

PROVERBS 15:1

Lyin' Eyes

Fata Morgana—Italian for Morgan le Fay, the sorceress in the legends of King Arthur—is a startling mirage that happens mostly at sea.[1] Though we now understand what causes it, historically the spooky apparition was blamed on the legendary enchantress.

A Fata Morgana requires a *thermal inversion*—a layer of cold, dense air trapped beneath a layer of warm, diffuse air. This happens most frequently at sea because the water (and the air in contact with it) is usually colder than the air higher up. Think of a sunny, spring day at the beach, when the air is warm but the water is cold.

Thermal inversions create a pathway—an *atmospheric duct*—along which light skimming the horizon can follow the earth's curvature, the same way light can follow the bend of a curved fiber-optic cable.

If you're at sea, a Fata Morgana enables the light from a very distant object—one that has already sunk well below the horizon—to travel up and around the earth's curvature right into your eyes. What's more, the image you see is distorted in an eerie way.

Typically, a Fata Morgana takes the actual image of the faraway object, flips it upside down, then stacks multiple copies of both upon each other. The result is an illusion that appears otherworldly.

Fata Morganas might be behind the legend of the *Flying Dutchman*—the famous ghost ship that sails aimlessly at sea, never able to dock. Sailors report seeing the marooned ship floating just above the horizon—just as you'd expect from a Fata Morgana. They also believe that spotting the apparition invariably signals impending doom.

Sailors also say that the *Dutchman* can suddenly vanish, right before their eyes. Because Fata Morganas depend on specific atmospheric conditions that can dissipate without warning, this aspect of the legend, too, fits perfectly with what we know about the supposed Arthurian witch's sorcery.

REFLECTION

Like a mirage, a lie takes the truth and distorts it. Moreover, the more fantastic the lie, the more attention it's liable to attract, even if it's eventually debunked.

According to the Bible, a fantastic lie is what led to the downfall of our species. It's why God booted us out of the heaven-on-Earth he created for us.

When Eve explained to the serpent that God had forbidden her and Adam from eating the fruit of one specific tree, on penalty of death, the serpent replied with a whopper: "You won't die! . . . God knows that your eyes will be opened as soon as you eat it, and you will be like God, knowing both good and evil."[2]

The serpent—whom the Bible calls "the father of lies"—was merely doing what came naturally. The actual tragedy was Eve's naive response to his deadly lie.

"The woman was convinced," the Bible reports. "She saw that the tree was beautiful and its fruit looked delicious, and she wanted the wisdom it would give her. So she took some of the fruit and ate it."[3]

You don't have to believe in the Bible for this story to ring true. Study after scientific study—together with everyday experience—affirms our species' notorious predilection to lie and our catastrophic inclination to believe lies.

Your only defense against falsehoods, which abound in today's Age of Misinformation, is to be doggedly skeptical of all significant claims. To ask tough questions and demand honest answers.

In short, your only defense against Eve-like naiveté—against a chronically lying species, an untrustworthy internet, and the Fata Morganas created by people with hidden agendas—is to *do your homework*.

THE CREATOR SPEAKS

My dear friends, don't believe everything you hear. Carefully weigh and examine what people tell you.
1 JOHN 4:1, MSG

The Good Shepherd

It has been estimated that there are more than one billion domesticated sheep in the world. That's easy to believe, given how much we depend on the fluffy creatures for meat, cheese, milk, wool, and leather.

Sheep are a fascinating study in contrasts.

On the one hand, they can behave quite intelligently. Faced with a cattle grate—parallel bars set on the ground across a gate opening and spaced such that a cow's (or sheep's) hooves can fall through—the sheep learned to cross the barrier by lying down and rolling over it.

On the other hand, sheep can behave quite stupidly. In 2005, while Turkish shepherds watched over their flock of 1,500 sheep, one of the animals wandered away to the edge of a nearby cliff, glanced down, and jumped to its death.

As if that weren't bad enough, the other sheep in the herd saw what happened and followed suit. One by one, the remaining 1,499 sheep jumped off the cliff.

The frantic shepherds tried to intervene, but they couldn't stop the mass suicide. Fortunately, after the first 400 or so sheep made the fatal leap, their dead bodies formed a cushion that softened the fall of the others, thus sparing their lives.

REFLECTION

The Bible frequently compares us to sheep—an apt comparison, given that we, like sheep, are a fascinating study in contrasts.

On the one hand, we're capable of behaving very intelligently. We've invented countless laborsaving devices, figured out some of nature's most obscure secrets, and even landed humans on the moon.

On the other hand, we're also capable of behaving stupidly. In 1992, Wendy Northcutt, a molecular biologist at Stanford, created the Darwin

Awards to recognize stellar feats of stupidity by her fellow humans. In her own words: "The Darwin Awards commemorate individuals who protect our gene pool by . . . eliminat[ing] themselves in an extraordinarily idiotic manner, thereby improving our species' chance of long-term survival."[1]

Our species' seemingly boundless capacity for utter and lethal foolishness, the Bible explains, is why we need a shepherd who loves us and never sleeps: *Jesus.* He's the Good Shepherd, who will brave any danger in order to rescue us from the huge messes we get into.

He is the Good Shepherd, who protects us from ourselves. From our natural, yet misguided predilection to go along with the masses—even if it means following them off a cliff.

THE CREATOR SPEAKS

If the blind lead the blind, both will fall into a pit.
MATTHEW 15:14, ESV

I am the good shepherd. The good shepherd sacrifices his life for the sheep.
JOHN 10:11

Vast and Wondrous

For most of human history, we've gazed up at the night sky and been awed by its vastness. We stare wondrously at the mysterious, colored points of light that nightly sail, silently and unerringly, from east to west.

For centuries, imaginative authors such as H. G. Wells and Jules Verne envisioned the day when we'd invent a cannon, rocket ship, ladder, or some other fanciful contraption that would allow us to travel among those points of light and inspect them up close. Then, at last, that day approached.

In 1947, the US sent fruit flies and corn seeds into space aboard a military V-2 sounding rocket. Two years later, the US sent up a rhesus monkey named Albert, who survived the trip but not the landing; tragically, his parachute failed to deploy.

In 1957, the Soviet Union launched a stray dog named Laika into space (she died in flight), followed by a man (Yuri Gagarin, 1961), and then a woman (Valentina Tereshkova, 1963).

In the 1960s, the US and the Soviet Union competed in an all-out *space race*, with each nation striving to build ever-bigger, ever-more-powerful rockets. The race culminated on July 16, 1969, when billions of people worldwide watched in awe and wonder as American astronaut Neil Armstrong set foot on the moon.

Most of today's young people take space travel for granted—unaware of the long, deadly journey that allowed our species to travel into space. The US–Soviet space race has been replaced by a race among billionaires who have their sights set on making fortunes by sending everyday people around the earth, to the moon, and even to Mars.

Within a mere decade, it's very likely that you, dear reader—yes, *you*—will have the opportunity to follow in the pioneering pathways of fruit flies, corn seeds, rhesus monkeys, and stray dogs. To travel, at last, among the mysterious points of colored lights that have fascinated and called out to us for thousands of years.

REFLECTION

Modern evolutionary biology encourages the belief that our species—any species, actually—is primarily motivated by a hardwired desire to perpetuate its gene pool. It's the central theme, for example, of Oxford scientist Richard Dawkins's bestselling book *The Selfish Gene.*

It's undeniable, of course, that we're motivated to save our own skin; no one wants to die. But it's also crystal clear we're willing to sacrifice our very lives to satisfy an even greater urge: our unique, dogged curiosity about everything and anything in the universe.

Our curiosity is flagrantly non-Darwinian. Being curious about the far side of the moon doesn't improve our chances of surviving here on Earth—just the opposite, it diminishes our chances by quite a lot, yet we don't care.

Even more brazenly non-Darwinian is this: We are curious about not just the natural world—not just the farthest reaches of outer space—but the vast and mysterious *supernatural* world as well. One example of our utter fascination with all things otherworldly is the popularity of the Bible, by far the most widely published and translated book in history.

So what does the Bible—God's very own words—say about all this?

According to it, the starry night sky is vast and wondrous for one simple, profound reason: It's the handiwork of a vast and wondrous creator. The self-same creator who made *you* wondrous . . . and your *curiosity* vast.

THE CREATOR SPEAKS

When I look at the night sky and see the work of your fingers—
the moon and the stars you set in place—
what are mere mortals that you should think about them,
human beings that you should care for them?
Yet you made them only a little lower than God
and crowned them with glory and honor.

PSALM 8:3-5

Sweet as Honey

Honeybees need to make enough honey to sustain their entire colony—upwards of 60,000 individuals—throughout the long winter season, when flowers are scarce. Lucky for us, they usually make two to three times *more* than that.

It's a monumental, arduous, complex achievement.

Bees roam up to four miles away from their hive to suck nectar from flowering plants; ingest it inside their stomachs, where it is thoroughly mixed with invertase and other enzymes; cram the watery, digested nectar into their hive's small, hexagonal wax cells; fan it with their wings until it evaporates down to a perfectly concentrated honey (from roughly a 75 percent water content to 18 percent); then finally cap each cellful of honey with a wax seal.

All in all, it takes eight to twelve honeybees their *entire lives* to make one teaspoon of honey. But the Herculean effort is more than worth it—for the bees *and* us.

Since the Stone Age, we've relied on this precious substance not only to sweeten our foods, but to heal our wounds. The medical papyri of ancient Egypt are filled with descriptions of honey-based remedies.

When honey is applied to a cut, for example, its low-water content helps keep the wound dry, and its trace amounts of hydrogen peroxide and acidic pH help keep the wound clean and disinfected by staving off bacteria and other pathogens.

Presently, scientists are exploring the possibility that honey made by stingless bees in Malaysia has strong antioxidant properties and might even be helpful in treating malignant gliomas, diabetes, and other serious illnesses.

REFLECTION

"Sticks and stones can break my bones, but words will never hurt me."

You probably grew up hearing that old saying, but it's simply not true. In truth, words have enormous power, either to sting like vinegar or soothe like honey.

Even a passing remark—from a teacher, loved one, or friend—can wound us deeply or encourage us greatly. That's why the Bible says it's so important to think before we speak.

In today's age of instant communication, that's harder to do than ever before. We text or type a message with rapidly moving thumbs and fingers and immediately—without a second thought—push Send.

Compared to the days of handwritten letters and snail mail, today we're more likely to speak before thinking. It's one reason why social media is causing so much harm.

Next time you open your mouth to say something—for example, to the young person bagging your groceries, the clerk at the bank, or to a parent or child—remember: What you say has the power to hurt or heal. Make certain your words are as healthful and helpful as honey.

THE CREATOR SPEAKS

Do not let any unwholesome talk come out of your mouths, but only what is helpful for building others up according to their needs, that it may benefit those who listen.
EPHESIANS 4:29, NIV

One in a Billion

Most bats live in large colonies, which offer the winged animals safety, warmth (generated by their collective body heat), and mutual care. The world's largest known colony of Mexican free-tailed bats (*Tadarida brasiliensis*) is located in Bracken Cave, near San Antonio, Texas.

Every summer more than twenty million bats fly to Bracken from Mexico, Central America, and northern South America to procreate. Once there, each adult female gives birth to a single pup, which instantly causes the colony's population to swell—so much so that it becomes the world's largest gathering of nonhuman, warm-blooded mammals.

To make room for the babies—all of whom roost on the cave's ceiling, where it is warmest—adult male bats vacate the premises. Their mass exodus leaves behind a huge noisy, messy maternity ward.

In the midst of all that chaos—with millions of babies crowded together at up to 500 per square foot—each mom has to be able to locate her one offspring. How in the world does she manage that? Biologists aren't sure, but they speculate that she's able to distinguish her baby's smell and voice, both of which are unique in extremely subtle ways.

For five weeks after giving birth, the Mexican free-tailed mothers hunt for food, then locate and nurse their newborn pups twice a day. After that, the pups leave the cave to hunt with their moms, creating so much air traffic it shows up on the radar screens of nearby airports.

At its peak, an estimated 50,000 mothers and babies soar out of Bracken Cave *every minute*. Even at that rate, this spectacular show lasts a full three hours.

REFLECTION

According to the latest census, there are more than eight billion people in the world, with roughly 140 million babies being born each year.[1] Yet, according to the Bible, God is able to recognize each person not only by smell and voice, but by the totality of the person's being.

The God described in the Bible can not only spot you in a crowd of billions, but he also loves you far more than a Mexican free-tailed bat mother loves her pup. He loves you as if you were the only person alive, and he desires for you to love him in return.

Before you can do that, however, you yourself must be able to recognize God. To single him out from among the chaos of other deities and idols that people worship.

You must be able to recognize that your creator, unlike any other being in and beyond the cosmos, is prepared to move heaven and earth to find you, embrace you, and care for you—not just for a season, but forever.

THE CREATOR SPEAKS

Can a mother forget her nursing child?
Can she feel no love for the child she has borne?
But even if that were possible,
I would not forget you!
ISAIAH 49:15

Dancing in the Dryness

The desert rhubarb (*Rheum palaestinum*) thrives in an environment deadly to most life-forms. Found high in the mountains of the Negev Desert across Israel and Jordan, its tall stalks sprout so many small, red flowers they seem to be ablaze with fire.

Each year, the Negev receives a paltry two to six inches of rain. The famous desert is so arid and so hot that two-thirds of the rainwater often evaporates before it even has a chance to penetrate the soil.

Plants living in the Negev typically have leaves or needles with small surface areas, the better to minimize evaporation. But not the desert rhubarb. Crowning its base, against all odds, are up to four huge leaves—each one about a foot-and-a-half across. For a long time, this stunning anomaly stumped scientists; but now, after years of intense research, they understand and marvel at the plant's miraculous design.

Each dark-green, plastic-like leaf has a waxy coating and is scored with wide grooves. The broad, waxy leaves collect precipitation and the grooves channel the rainwater in a way that optimally waters the plant's main stem.

Because this brilliant self-irrigation system is so effective, the rhubarb's roots receive about *sixteen times* more water than the roots of desert plants all around it. In a light rain that doesn't even wet the ground, the desert rhubarb still manages to water itself.

The scientists who made these discoveries are from Israel's University of Haifa at Oranim. To them, the desert rhubarb's design is truly a wonder to behold: "We know of no other plant in the deserts of the world that functions in this manner."[1]

REFLECTION

There are times in life when it can feel as if we're living in the middle of a desert, desperately trying to survive. Whether it's a treasured relationship, our finances, our plans for the future, or our sense of joy that has shriveled up and died, we're left wondering if it's ever going to rain hope again.

During such times, God wants us to cry out to him for help. But beware: He doesn't always answer right away. Just ask Job.

What then?

In such times, remember the desert rhubarb. Like that miraculous plant, you are designed with a brilliant, built-in, self-irrigation system called *thanksgiving*.

Like oversized leaves, your arms open wide to collect your many, overlooked blessings; and through prayer, you channel them in a way that waters your soul. Simply by giving thanks, you magnify the effectiveness of what little rain you're presently receiving.

While others trudging through their own deserts are at the end of their rope, ready to give up and die, you are nourished by a sincere attitude of gratitude. It's a unique strategy that empowers you not only to survive, but actually to celebrate during life's most severe droughts.

THE CREATOR SPEAKS

Always be joyful. Never stop praying. Be thankful in all circumstances.

1 THESSALONIANS 5:16-18

Straighten Up and Fly Right

In 1835, Gaspard-Gustave de Coriolis, a young French mathematician, was the first to publish an explanation of the strange thing that happens whenever you try traveling in a straight line. If you live in the Northern Hemisphere, you inevitably veer to the right. If you live in the Southern Hemisphere, you inescapably and mysteriously veer to the left.

This perplexing phenomenon, Coriolis explained, is an illusion caused by our earthly perspective. When we set out to go straight, we tend to forget the ground beneath us is constantly shifting, owing to Earth's spin.

If a plane in Chicago takes off in the direction of New York City, it will never arrive there, because during the journey, New York City has rotated out of position by several hundred miles. In order to reach its destination, therefore, the plane must follow a curved path, not a straight one.

Today we call this simple but confounding principle the Coriolis effect. And we now recognize its widespread significance.

In the military, for example, the Coriolis effect skews the trajectories of long-range munitions. During World War I, the Germans bombarding Paris from seventy miles away needed to adjust the aim of their Big Bertha guns by nearly a mile in order to strike the intended target.

In meteorology, the Coriolis effect is what causes straight air currents to veer right or left. In severe cases, the arching air currents develop into full-fledged hurricanes, typhoons, cyclones, and anticyclones.

Above all, we now understand that to someone whose perspective is not of this earth, the Coriolis effect doesn't exist. From their lofty perspective, planes seemingly curving toward their destinations, bombs curving toward their targets, and air currents curving in Coriolis-like ways—are, in fact, all moving in *straight* lines!

REFLECTION

Your worldview, your personal point of view, guides your every decision; yet it isn't always reliable. It routinely deceives you and keeps you from getting to where you want to go.

It's as if you're under the influence of your very own Coriolis effect. You set out in life with a dream and start working toward it, only to find that you've missed the mark. Maybe by a lot.

Naturally, you can become discouraged, and after many years of failure, quit trying.

Please don't! Instead, pause and recalibrate your heading. Take into account that your perception of *straight* is not the same as God's.

Allow for the possibility that, from God's lofty perspective, you're aiming at the wrong target.

Allow for the possibility that your lifelong dream isn't what's best for you—and might even be what's worst for you.

Allow for the possibility that your long, circuitous journey in life is actually taking you precisely to where God lovingly and purposely wants you to go.

THE CREATOR SPEAKS

Seek his will in all you do, and he will show you which path to take.
PROVERBS 3:6

Resemblance

No doubt you've heard that humans and chimps have genomes that are 98.7 percent identical. The point is often made by people arguing against human exceptionalism.

Our universe is volatile; its behavior is *chaotic*. It's a world where tiny differences can have outsized consequences (see Invitation 92).

It isn't surprising, therefore, that human and chimp genomes are similar. And that the 1.3 percent difference between them has profound significance.

Even more dramatic are the differences among human genomes alone.

The DNAs of everyone who has ever lived, is currently alive, and will ever live are *99.9 percent* identical! Yet that seemingly insignificant 0.1 percent dissimilarity is entirely responsible for humankind's dazzling diversity.

REFLECTION

The remarkable similarity among the DNAs of all life on Earth is precisely what you'd expect if everything were the product of a brilliant, efficient creator. If, from the beginning, God designed a single long molecule with the potential of becoming everything from a sponge to a spider, a trilobite to a tomato, a hummingbird to a human being.

He designed a molecule so economical that tiny changes are able to produce the entire panoply of plants and animals that walk, swim, and fly on our planet. It's a molecule so ingenious, so powerful that it would take longer than the age of the universe for blind chance to piece it together—a likelihood akin to birds producing Shakespeare's *Hamlet* by pecking randomly on a keyboard; or chimps producing Leonardo da Vinci's *Mona Lisa* by splashing colored paints on a canvas.

Think about that every time you ooh and aah at the spectacular biodiversity of our planet. And at the monumental differences between chimps and humans, despite their near-identical DNAs.

THE CREATOR SPEAKS

All things came into being through Him, and apart from Him nothing came into being.
JOHN 1:3, NASB

33

Detox Program

The most poisonous frogs in the world live in Central and South America. They're called poison dart frogs (family Dendrobatidae) because for centuries indigenous hunters smeared their blowgun darts with the frogs' poison to bring down large prey, including jaguars and monkeys.

As is often the case with toxic plants and animals, poison dart frogs are brightly colored. The skin of the Harlequin variety of the frogs (*Oophaga histrionica*), for instance, is dappled with more than thirty dazzling, neon-like hues.

Golden poison dart frogs (*Phyllobates terribilis*), which live in the lowland rain forests of Colombia, are the most lethal of all. A single frog—roughly the size of a paper clip—carries enough poison on its skin to kill ten full-grown men on contact.

One of the more astonishing features of the poison dart frog is that it isn't poisonous by nature. Its toxicity isn't genetic. Rather, its extreme deadliness comes from its steady diet of poisonous insects. The poison builds up inside the frog's tiny body and oozes out of its skin.

When poison dart frogs feed on nonpoisonous foods—as they do in most zoos—they lose their toxicity. They become as harmless as ordinary frogs!

REFLECTION

According to the Bible, we are genetically predisposed to rebel against God. It's the fallen nature we've inherited from our common ancestors, dating back to Noah's family, who themselves inherited it from Adam and Eve.

Despite that, however, there is a very practical way for you to keep your fallen nature in check. Cut back on the poisons you ingest from what you listen to, watch, and think about—poisons that inevitably ooze out of you.

Yes, it's not easy to change diets. But the Bible explains: Choose constantly to be mindful of God, and your appetite for good things will automatically increase—for entertainment that inspires; relationships that lift you up, not tear you down; ambitions that are in line with—not hostile to—God's will for your life.

Don't put it off. The time to detoxify your diet is now.

THE CREATOR SPEAKS

And now, dear brothers and sisters, one final thing. Fix your thoughts on what is true, and honorable, and right, and pure, and lovely, and admirable. Think about things that are excellent and worthy of praise. . . . Then the God of peace will be with you.

PHILIPPIANS 4:8-9

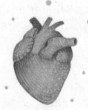

Hitchhiking
through Life

Unlike conventional volcanoes, whose eruptions are easy to behold, those on the bottom of the ocean often go off without anyone noticing. Sometimes the only evidence we can see of these stealthy, underwater eruptions are what we call *pumice rafts*.

Pumice is a coarse, volcanic rock riddled with cavities, like a sponge. The tiny voids trap gases that make pumice extremely buoyant.

An underwater volcanic eruption typically produces huge amounts of pumice—trillions of rocks as small as marbles and big as human skulls. When all that material breaches, it tends to aggregate into massive, floating rafts that blanket large areas of the ocean's surface.

From late December 2021 to January 15, 2022, one such underwater volcano erupted three times in the South Pacific. Currently ranked as this century's largest eruption, it produced a pumice raft nearly *20 square miles* in size.[1]

Unbelievably, in the great scheme of things, that's considered small.

In 2019, an underwater eruption in the Southwest Pacific, which no one noticed, produced a pumice raft that was more than twice as big—fifty-eight square miles. Even larger was the 154-square-mile pumice raft caused by the 2012 eruption of an underwater volcano named Havre, in the Kermadec Arc, north of New Zealand—a blast one and a half times the size of the Mount St. Helens eruption.[2]

Pumice rafts can be as much as a foot thick, which poses a very real danger to ships at sea. At the very least, encountering one is an eerie, unpleasant experience. The normally blue ocean and fresh air instantly give way to a vast gray wasteland of drifting pumice that smells like rotten eggs (sulfur dioxide).

For some species, however, pumice rafts can prove to be an unexpected blessing. In 2006, an enormous pumice raft sailed thousands of miles across the Pacific Ocean for eight long months. During that time, more than eighty kinds of anemone, barnacle, coral, mollusk, and crab hopped aboard the passing raft and rode it all the way to Australia's Great Barrier Reef!

REFLECTION

We've all heard about the dangers of hitchhiking; but the truth is, we're all hitchhikers. There's no avoiding it.

We advance in life not just by our own efforts, but by the kindness of others. People we meet—and in many cases, never meet—offer a helping hand of some kind.

It can be a glowing job recommendation, a break in life for which we've been waiting, or an introduction to someone who opens doors for us. Whatever it is, the kindness—like a pumice raft—constitutes a free ride from point A to point B.

But don't forget: The reverse is also true. There are times when you can be someone's else life raft. Why not be that for someone today? Someone who's adrift at sea, waiting—praying desperately—for a much-needed lift.

THE CREATOR SPEAKS

The generous will prosper;
those who refresh others will themselves be refreshed.
PROVERBS 11:25

A Lush Relationship

In the high mountains of eastern New Guinea, you'll find various members of a very unusual family of true weevils (family Curculionidae) crawling among the leaf litter. The weevils are hard to spot because they're small—the largest one only about an inch-and-a-half long—and because miniature forests growing on their backs help mask their presence.

Amazingly, just like the vast mossy, humid forest the weevils call home, their tiny "backpack" forests are teeming with life. Not just tiny plant life—for example, mosses, lichens, liverworts, and baby ferns—but other tiny life-forms such as mites, nematodes, and bacteria, as well.

It all begins with the sticky, mucosal ridges on the weevil's shell. These ridges are very effective at catching hold of spores, pollen, mites, and other minuscule plant and animal material blowing in the wind.

Because the weevils don't move very fast or very far, and because they live a relatively long time—up to five years—the progenitors of their tiny forests aren't easily shaken off. They have plenty of time to mature into full-fledged, miniature, arboreal ecosystems.

Scientists call this rare phenomenon *epizoic symbiosis*, a fancy way of describing a mutually beneficial relationship between plants and animals. The weevils offer plants (and their tiny animal companions) a safe space to thrive; the plants, in turn, provide weevils with lifesaving camouflage.

REFLECTION

The concept that a mere mortal can have a personal relationship with the spiritual being who created the universe is phenomenal—some might say beyond belief. Yet it's at the very core of the Christian worldview.

In its own way, this core concept is akin to the epizoic symbiosis between New Guinean weevils and the forest life they tote on their tiny backs. In the case of Christianity, however, it's God who totes us on his back.

Also according to the Christian worldview, God will never force himself on you. You must choose to climb aboard and then remain there with sincerity and perseverance.

If you do that—if you hop aboard and hang on—the experiences you'll have atop God's back will forever change your life. In return, God will revel in your love for and trust in him.

THE CREATOR SPEAKS

No eye has seen, no ear has heard,
  and no mind has imagined
what God has prepared
  for those who love him.
1 CORINTHIANS 2:9

Deadly Attraction

Imagine yourself as a hungry insect crawling or flying around the woodlands of North and South Carolina, desperately looking for something to eat. At long last, you come to a flower dripping with nectar.

Jackpot!

Or so you think. In reality, you've stumbled upon a deadly Venus flytrap (*Dionaea muscipula*), a rare carnivorous plant that eats insects.

Its exotic flower resembles an open mouth lined with spines called cilia. The cilia are bathed in a sweet, fragrant liquid that lures unsuspecting insects to step inside.

When an insect enters the trap, it triggers tiny, black hairs inside the flower's mouth and throat. If two or more hairs are triggered within a twenty-second window, they electrically signal the Venus flytrap to close up—but only loosely. If additional hairs are triggered, the jaws clamp down hard. If not, the flower treats the event like a false alarm and opens up again.

Once the victim is securely confined, the flower releases a deadly cocktail of acids and digestive juices. Over the course of several days, these powerful fluids liquefy the insect into a nutrient-rich broth, which the Venus flytrap feeds on for a week.

Once the feast is fully consumed, the Venus flytrap opens its deadly mouth once again and lies in wait for its next unsuspecting meal.

REFLECTION

For us humans, money has the same strong appeal as nectar does for insects. We are easily conned into believing it's the answer to all our problems.

Hit the lottery and you'll be happy for the rest of your life, right?

Wrong. Studies find that if you're unhappy before striking it rich, then following a brief period of euphoria, you'll return to being unhappy.

Hitting the jackpot also invites into your life all kinds of untoward solicitations from friends, family, and outright strangers, as well as all kinds of unhealthy temptations.

Entire business enterprises, not just individuals, are also vulnerable to the sweet smell and taste of money. When corporations become successful, their leaders' priorities can easily devolve to valuing profits above the wellbeing of their employees and customers.

The Bible makes clear that money alone, like nectar alone, isn't toxic. Earned honestly and spent wisely it can help enormous numbers of people in great need.

The problem is when you covet money—valuing it above anything and anyone else in your life. That's when it comes with spines, hair triggers, and jaws that will entrap and ultimately destroy you.

THE CREATOR SPEAKS

But people who long to be rich fall into temptation and are trapped by many foolish and harmful desires that plunge them into ruin and destruction. For the love of money is the root of all kinds of evil. And some people, craving money, have wandered from the true faith and pierced themselves with many sorrows.
1 TIMOTHY 6:9-10

The Sound of Prayer

Of the thirty-six species of dolphin (order Cetacea), some live in fresh-water streams and rivers, while most inhabit the world's salty oceans. All, however, have one powerful ability in common: *echolocation*.

Using *phonic lips*—a very special organ in their blowholes—dolphins emit a rapid-fire mix of clicks, trills, moans, grunts, whistles, and squeaks that fan out through the water at 3,240 miles per hour. The sounds bounce off everything in their way, and the dolphins translate the echoes into a very detailed, mental picture of their surroundings.

These echolocation maps enable dolphins to perceive the shape, com-position, position, size, distance, and direction of all nearby objects. And they're precise enough to perceive objects a mere quarter-inch across.

Combined with what dolphins can actually see with their eyes, these sound maps make it possible for the cetaceans to hunt and swim in extremely deep water, in regions of the ocean that are literally pitch black due to a complete absence of sunlight.

REFLECTION

You don't have a crystal clear view of life. You're like a creature swimming through murky waters, wondering: *Who am I? What's my purpose? What's the best next step? What job should I take? Where should I live? Whom should I marry?* And on and on.

The good news is that, like a dolphin, you have the powerful ability to echolocate. Instead of phonic lips that send out sonic waves, you have lips that send out spiritual waves, also known as *prayers*.

A proper prayer to God doesn't ask for things you want: You aren't supposed to be like a kid asking Santa Claus for Christmas gifts. A proper prayer is like a series of clicks, moans, and squeaks—a heartfelt plea for clarity about what's happening to you and all around you.

If your entire being is properly receptive—body, mind, heart, and spirit—you will hear not only the echoes of your own voice pleading for help, but also God's voice. His still, small voice will paint a revealing map for you to follow.

It will help you navigate through life's murkiest waters. But only if you pray properly . . . and listen attentively.

THE CREATOR SPEAKS

Ask me and I will tell you remarkable secrets you do not know about things to come.
JEREMIAH 33:3

If you need wisdom, ask our generous God, and he will give it to you. He will not rebuke you for asking.
JAMES 1:5

Musical Universe

Throughout history, people have discovered reasons to believe the universe is fundamentally musical. That it sings to us, even if we can't hear it.

One such person was Pythagoras, the ancient Greek philosopher and mathematician. He's most famous for the Pythagorean theorem, a handy mathematical formula concerning right triangles that you probably learned in geometry class.

Pythagoras also concocted an ancient cosmology known as *music of the spheres*. According to this idea, the seven main celestial bodies known in his day—the sun, moon, and five planets (Mercury, Venus, Mars, Jupiter, Saturn)—correspond to the seven musical notes of the Western diatonic musical scale: A, B, C, D, E, F, G.

That ancient cosmology has come and gone, but interestingly enough, it has been replaced by a similar-minded, modern cosmology known as *string theory*. This new idea was first proposed in the 1970s, and it remains a subject of great fascination.

According to the most popular version of string theory, the tiniest pixels of physical reality are 10D strings of space-time—nine dimensions of space, one of time. Moreover, it claims that these 10D strings *vibrate*—they sing with voices that are *seen*, not heard.

According to this novel cosmology, the strings' different voices correspond to the different known subatomic particles. Put more poetically, string theorists—reminiscent of Pythagoras before them—envision the universe as a magnificent, celestial choir of quantum-sized vocalists.

REFLECTION

According to the Bible, cosmologists from Pythagoras to now are on the right track. When God created the universe, he didn't wave a magic wand. Instead, he spoke, or—if you wish—sang it into existence.

From its smallest to its largest levels, there is a music-like harmony to the natural world, God's creation. Electron clouds gyrate around nuclei of protons and neutrons in rhythmic ways choreographed by the laws of quantum mechanics. Moons circle planets, and planets circle the sun with different and distinctive frequencies, governed by the law of gravity.

These powerful cadences resound throughout creation. We behold it in a sunflower tracking the sun across the sky; the rise and fall of the tides, mirroring the lunar cycle; and birds nesting in perfect step with the seasons.

Every single rhythm is an echo of God's voice. Stop and listen to what's around you, and you'll hear the creator singing the universe into existence.

THE CREATOR SPEAKS

For everything there is a season,
*   a time for every activity under heaven.*
A time to be born and a time to die.
*   A time to plant and a time to harvest, . . .*
A time to cry and a time to laugh.
*   A time to grieve and a time to dance.*
ECCLESIASTES 3:1-2, 4

Thar She Blows!

For a very long time, scientists believed that *all* life—not just photo-synthetic plant life—needed sunlight to exist, either directly or indi-rectly. In 1977, however, that dogma was demolished by the discovery of hydrothermal vents at the bottom of the Pacific Ocean.

These hydrothermal vents are thunderous geysers of seawater powered by magma welling up from deep within the earth's crust. The super-heated seawater is so hot—up to 750°F—it can melt solid metal.

Shockingly, marine biologists have discovered that hydrothermal vents are not entirely deadly as they initially thought. In reality, the vents are awesome, majestic, improbable fountains of life.

Among the strangest of all are the giant tubeworms (*Riftia pachyptila*)—long white annelids adorned with large, red-and-pink petals that group together in ways that resemble otherworldly, under-water gardens. Hydrothermal vent communities also teem with snails, limpets, giant clams, white crabs, rare fish species, and eyeless shrimp—more than 500 species have been identified so far.

None of these exotic life-forms will ever see sunlight, much less depend on it; instead, they thrive because of nutrifying minerals spew-ing from Earth's crust. Copious amounts of copper, iron, zinc, lead, and various sulfides precipitate out when the superheated vent water collides with the ice-cold ocean water—feeding the hydrothermal zoo and adding a dazzling rainbow of colors to the lively, unlikely scene.

REFLECTION

There are times when anger, bitterness, and resentment get the better of us. Often it's because something has been eating away at us for a long time and suddenly a last straw causes us to erupt like a hydrothermal vent.

At that point we are in a very dark place, fuming with emotions so hot they could melt solid metal.

What happens next?

On the one hand, we could take out our anger on everyone around us, maybe even on God. But the consequences won't be pretty.

On the other hand, we could offer up our anger to God, asking him to take it from us. The consequences of that will be a positive game changer.

By replacing your anger with God's peace, your deadly eruptions can become a fountain of life. Your anger, bitterness, and resentment can be channeled in positive ways that will help you cool off, and even help others who themselves are about to erupt.

THE CREATOR SPEAKS

Do not let the sun go down while you are still angry, and do not give the devil a foothold.... Get rid of all bitterness, rage and anger, brawling and slander, along with every form of malice.
EPHESIANS 4:26-27, 31, NIV

The Long Haul

The bird with the longest wings on earth—the wandering albatross (*Diomedea exulans*)—is built for endurance. With a wingspan of more than eleven feet, it lives entirely in and around the Antarctic.

The adversities it must endure in life begin at birth. Given its cold, harsh surroundings, a baby albatross is slow to develop. It can take up to ten months for it to fledge, at which point it flies out to sea, where it spends many years fully maturing. It eats krill, squid, and cuttlefish; sleeps on the water; and is one of very few nonaquatic animals that can desalinate and drink seawater.

A young male albatross spends up to ten years out at sea, growing strong and learning his species' extremely complex mating ritual. Once he's fully mature, he returns to the land, where—if he has successfully mastered his species' song-and-dance routine—he lands himself a mate for life.

When an albatross couple conceive, they usually produce only a single egg. The two parents feed and protect their little hatchling, until—many months later—it has enough feathers and know-how to take off on its own, destined to repeat the species' demanding lifecycle.

During its entire lifetime—typically fifty years or more—an albatross soars for thousands of miles over the rough seas of the Southern Hemisphere, without once flapping its wings, facing cold, unrelenting, howling forty- and fifty-mile-per-hour winds.[1]

It returns to land—usually a cold, windswept island—about once every two years. When it arrives, it seeks out and reunites with its beloved mate, and together they produce another chick.

REFLECTION

There will be times in your life when you feel as if you are running on empty. Perhaps you're feeling that way right now. Maybe it's because you're overworked or over-lonely or overextended financially.

During such times, think of the albatross flying alone in the cold, windy Antarctic, with nowhere to land except the wave-swept surface of a steel-gray, unforgiving ocean. Just as the albatross is built for endurance, in a sense so are you—even though it may not feel that way when you're flying on fumes.

God gave the albatross a mighty set of wings and an ocean of food. Likewise, he has given you a mighty spirit and an ocean of love. But without availing yourself of these resources, you cannot survive—any more than an albatross can survive without the resources God has given it.

Whatever challenges you now face will only be made worse by trying to go it alone. Rouse your mighty spirit, accept God's ocean of love, and like the amazing albatross you will grow in maturity, confidence, and your ability to endure.

THE CREATOR SPEAKS

We can rejoice, too, when we run into problems and trials, for we know that they help us develop endurance. And endurance develops strength of character, and character strengthens our confident hope of salvation. And this hope will not lead to disappointment.
ROMANS 5:3-5

E Pluribus Unum

Something wondrous and unique exists in the northern part of South America. More than fifteen thousand streams and rivers come together to form the single largest river in the world: the mighty Amazon.

During the peak of the dry season, the Amazon is only two miles wide. But during the wet season—from January to March—the collective flow from all those tributaries expands the width of the Amazon to a whopping *forty* miles!

The vast region crisscrossed by the Amazon's multitudinous streams and rivers—equal in size to the continental United States—is called the Amazon Basin. It sustains not only thirty million diverse peoples, but countless species of flora and fauna.

Scientists estimate that fully a third of the world's plant species live in the Amazon Basin. These include roughly eighty thousand species of trees and fifty-five thousand species of flowering plants.

So fecund is the Amazon Basin, in fact, that scientists speculate there are more fish species living in the streams, rivers, and main branch of the Amazon than in the entire Atlantic Ocean.

REFLECTION

Like the streams and rivers of the Amazon Basin, a multitude of small but persistent, faith-filled prayers are powerful. They are our lifeline to God, who has the power to level mountains of distress.

When your private petitions are joined by the fervent prayers of other Christians, the results can even trigger the revival of an entire nation. That's why the Bible urges us to set aside our selfish desires and petty differences and become unified in our requests to God.

If you ever find yourself doubting the power of collective, selfless prayer, remember the streams and rivers that give life to the Amazon

Basin. Each of them is important and powerful; but by coming together into one unified, mighty river, they help shape, design, and sustain the better part of an entire continent.

THE CREATOR SPEAKS

If two of you agree here on earth concerning anything you ask, my Father in heaven will do it for you. For where two or three gather together as my followers, I am there among them.
MATTHEW 18:19-20

The Journey

Each spring, roughly one hundred million monarch butterflies (*Danaus plexippus*) leave their wintering grounds—primarily in Mexico, Florida, and Southern California—and head northward. The journey is so long—many hundreds, even thousands, of miles—that the butterflies die along the way and their offspring must complete it.

When those offspring arrive at the monarch's northern breeding grounds—primarily the northeastern United States and southern Canada—they spend a busy summer procreating. During that time, second-, third-, and even fourth-generation offspring are born.

Come September, the fourth-generation offspring—the great-, great-grandchildren of the original migrants—feel a call to leave home and journey southward, back to the monarch's wintering grounds.

For eastern monarchs—those that live east of the Rockies—the journey is three thousand miles long. And their wintering grounds are just a few, very specific mountaintops in the Oyamel Forest of central Mexico.

There, in the branches of the forest's fir trees, the exhausted fourth-generation offspring huddle together against the cold, forming bulbous clusters resembling huge, black-and-orange Christmas ornaments. One cluster might hold as many as fifteen thousand butterflies.

Each monarch weighs less than a paper clip. But in some cases, the weight of a cluster is enough to snap off the branch it's hanging from.

How do monarchs manage to so precisely navigate such long distances back and forth? We have many theories that involve the sun's polarized light, Earth's magnetic field, and landmarks along the way—but, truthfully, we don't know.

How do the eastern monarchs' fourth-generation offspring know to overwinter specifically on those few mountaintops in central Mexico, when they've never been there before? Again, we have theories, but we don't know.

To this day, the migration of the monarchs remains a deep, scientific mystery.

REFLECTION

Your life is a journey; but is it well directed? Do you know exactly where you're going?

If you're like most people, the answer is *no*. By contrast, however, there are many people described in the Bible whose answer was a resounding *yes*.

One such person is Paul, a zealous Hebrew who became a devout Christian after experiencing an epiphany on his way to Damascus, the capital city of Syria. From that moment on—like a monarch butterfly— he knew exactly where he was going in life and why.

Paul didn't have wings and there were no trains, planes, or automobiles in his day, so he walked or rode ships the entire way. He journeyed more than ten thousand miles, through many nations—from Israel to Syria, Cyprus, Turkey, Greece, Italy, and possibly even Spain.

Along the way he endured great hardships—including many imprisonments and three shipwrecks—but also unspeakable joys. At the end of his long journey, though he was executed—reportedly beheaded in Rome at the command of the Christophobic Emperor Nero—he arrived at his mountaintop-like destination, fully contented.

How about you? Will you be able to claim the same thing at the end of your journey?

THE CREATOR SPEAKS

I have fought the good fight, I have finished the race . . . now the prize awaits me—the crown of righteousness.

2 TIMOTHY 4:7-8

Narrow Minds Think Alike

For many centuries, most people scoffed at stories dating back to ancient Greece about something called *blood rain*. In the *Iliad*, written in the eighth century BC, Homer describes an impending battle between the Trojans and the Achaeans: "The son of Cronos roused an evil din, and down from on high from out of heaven he sent dew-drops dank with blood, for that he was about to send forth to Hades many a valiant head."[1]

It was meant as a portent of the slaughter to come.

Dozens of accounts of blood rain were written throughout the Middle Ages and European Renaissance. But did they really happen? Absent any verifiable evidence, people understandably dismissed the reports as apocryphal—the colorful delusions of superstitious minds.

But then, during the summer of 2001, the residents of Kerala, a coastal city in southern India, were showered with blood rain. The crimson-colored precipitation continued for several weeks, staining everything it fell on.

This was no delusion, no superstition. The blood rain falling on Kerala was real and lingered long enough for government scientists to collect plenty of samples.

Following the analyses, the Indian government blamed the rain on a meteoric explosion. They claimed the blast contaminated clouds throughout the region, producing the reddish rain.

But that pronouncement didn't hold up to further scrutiny and was promptly abandoned.

On second thought, scientists said, the phenomenon was caused by red-colored spores, traces of which they'd found in the rain samples. But this explanation, too, fell apart upon further analysis.

On third thought, scientists said, Kerala's blood rain was caused by dust from nearby deserts. But further tests ruled out desert dust as a viable explanation.

In 2015, a team of Austrian and Indian scientists revisited the spore explanation, except this time they blamed it not on local spores, but on ones from faraway Europe. They hypothesized the spores were somehow carried to India by high atmospheric winds.

We might never know what caused Kerala's weeks-long rain of terror, but this much we do know: The phenomenon known as blood rain is real. The scoffers and skeptics were wrong.

REFLECTION

In the centuries leading up to today's scientific age, we've become quite full of ourselves. We believe that, given enough time, we'll be able to explain away every mystery in the universe.

But such self-assurance is not supported by the evidence. Look critically at the history of science and you'll see that every question the scientific method answers invariably raises hundreds of new questions we can't answer.

The unresolved saga of blood rain should humble us all. It shows that, for all our scientific perspicacity, we can't solve even a simple mystery close to home, never mind those of the far-flung universe—and least of all, the ultimate mystery: God, the *creator* of the universe.

You're free to scoff at the God of the Bible, of course, but be careful. The history of human experience—including the blood rain of Kerala—clearly reveals that our narrow-minded sense of what's possible or not possible is not a reliable indicator of what's actually possible or not possible.

THE CREATOR SPEAKS

Most importantly, I want to remind you that in the last days scoffers will come, mocking the truth and following their own desires.
2 PETER 3:3

In the Clouds

You've heard of rain forests and maybe even dry forests. But have you ever heard of cloud forests? They comprise just one percent of the planet's arboreal habitats.

Cloud forests are rare because they exist only in very specific settings: in tropical climates, high on the sides of mountains facing an ocean. Moist winds from the sea, driven upward by the mountain, condense into clouds that envelop the high-altitude forest nearly all the time.

The leaves of the forest's tallest trees snatch moisture from those clouds, forming droplets of water that rain down on the exotic trees, plants, and animals below. This manufactured rain—called fog drip—supplements the normal rainfall and keeps the forest thriving.

Cloud forests—for example, the famous Monteverde cloud forest along the Costa Rican coast—are home to a wide variety of extraordinary flora and fauna, much of which exist nowhere else. Countless orchids, ferns, begonias, and epiphytes—"air plants" rooted not in soil, but in tree trunks and branches high above the forest floor—revel in the warm, humid, shady paradise. They flourish so greatly, in fact, that some of the flowering plants grow as big as trees.

Andean bears, howler monkeys, tapirs, two-toed sloths, coatis, ocelots, and margays are just a few of the magnificent mammals that live in the clouds. Decorating the warm, dusky air are many different, scene-stealing butterflies, damselflies, bats, and wildly colorful birds. These include toucans, hummingbirds, and the elusive, legendary quetzal.

Cloaked in shimmering red, blue, green, and white feathers, the quetzal is considered by many to be the most beautiful bird in the world. The males are especially breathtaking, because their sleek twin tails can grow to be three feet long.

REFLECTION

Beyond even the highest clouds, a heavenly world awaits you. But whether you ever see or inhabit it is up to you. It's your choice.

Here on Earth, hiking up to a cloud forest takes quite an effort; you need to be in great shape.

By contrast, getting to spend eternity with God takes only a sincere, heartfelt decision; you don't even need to be in great shape.

Quite often, in fact, people who make the fateful decision are in the worst spiritual shape of their lives. It's precisely then that they see most clearly their need for help from someone or something not of their base world—someone who dwells high above even the highest paradise on Earth.

The cloud forest is known for its exotic beauty. Heaven is known for that as well—but truthfully, two-toed sloths and quetzals have nothing on angels. Or on God.

Hoping and praying to see you there.

THE CREATOR SPEAKS

For it is my Father's will that all who see his Son and believe in him should have eternal life. I will raise them up at the last day.
JOHN 6:40

Why Math?

In the movie *Peggy Sue Got Married*, a grown-up Peggy Sue magically goes back in time to her senior year of high school. When her math teacher scolds her for leaving a test question blank, she rises up and says to him: "Mr. Snelgrove, I happen to know that in the future I will not have the slightest use for algebra. And I speak from experience."[1]

Notwithstanding Peggy Sue's remonstration, mathematics has actually proven to be extremely useful in our efforts to figure out how the universe works. So much so, in fact, it raises many deep questions.

For example, the transcendental number pi plays a key role in population genetics. By definition, pi is the ratio of a circle's circumference to its diameter. Why in the world is an abstract number so relevant to populations of people and animals?

Then there's the so-called Fibonacci series: 0, 1, 1, 2, 3, 5, 8, 13, 21, 34, 55, 89, 144, 233, 377, 610, 987, and so forth. Each number in the sequence is the sum of the two numbers before it.

These numbers—credited to a thirteenth-century Italian mathematician named Leonardo da Pisa, aka Fibonacci—perfectly describe the number of: petals in many flowers, such as daisies; seeds in a sunflower; scales in a pinecone; and leaves in an aloe plant.

Moreover, Fibonacci numbers describe a spiral we see everywhere in nature. It's the shape of a fiddlehead fern, the ovary of an anglerfish, the curl of a chameleon's tail, the swirl of a hurricane's winds, the whorls in a fingerprint, and on and on.

Why are a bunch of totally abstract numbers, series, and equations so good at describing the real, physical world? What does it imply about our world and how it came to be?

For centuries, scientists and philosophers have struggled unsuccessfully to answer those vexing questions. In 1960, this impasse led the famous mathematician Eugene Wigner to say, "The enormous usefulness of mathematics in the natural sciences is something bordering on the mysterious and . . . there is no rational explanation for it."[2]

REFLECTION

The Bible and science agree that order and reason saturate the natural world. Earth, for instance, circles the sun in a way that obeys strict rules, including the law of gravity.

What's more, the Bible explains that this uncanny, mathematical orderliness is not an accident. It's the stunning manifestation of God's ineffable genius.

That's why we're so often at a loss for words to describe the natural world, his creation. We're left speechless by the beauty of a sunset, of a tropical bird such as a quetzal, or of a snowcapped mountain range such as the Colorado Rockies.

Words are utterly incapable of describing the elegant behavior of a spiral galaxy, the complex structure of a snowflake, or the magical properties of a DNA molecule.

These are the handiwork of a creator whose brilliance is beyond words. A brilliance only mathematics is able to capture—and even then, only roughly, because God is not just deeply rational, he's profoundly *translogical*. His inestimable mind defies not only words, but simple-minded mathematical logic as well.

THE CREATOR SPEAKS

Where were you when I laid the foundations of the earth?
    Tell me, if you know so much.
Who determined its dimensions
    and stretched out the surveying line?
What supports its foundations,
    and who laid its cornerstone
as the morning stars sang together
    and all the angels shouted for joy?

JOB 38:4-7

Darkness and Light

One bright, sunny morning in May 1780, the skies over New England suddenly turned spooky shades of yellow. Then abruptly everything went dark.

It's called New England's Dark Day, but in actuality the darkness extended beyond New England to parts of Canada.

George Washington wrote about it in his diary. Nathan Reed, a student at Harvard College, described each passing moment of the bizarre event for posterity.

Schools shut down, people left work, and the entire region was thrown into a panic. Believing that the darkness signaled the end of the world, many people desperately called for prayer and repentance.

By the next morning, everything was back to normal. The sun rose bright and clear in the east, and people resumed their normal routines.

In 1886, a similar episode of sudden darkness befell Oshkosh, Wisconsin—more sudden even than the darkness in New England. Within just five minutes, the city went from being bright and sunny to dark as midnight.

People sprinted into their cellars, businesses closed, and the entire population of Oshkosh held its collective breath in anticipation. Within ten minutes, the darkness dissipated and people emerged from their hiding places.

Scientists offer many possible explanations for these sudden episodes of darkness. They might be caused by sudden, massive forest fires whose thick smoke blocks out the sun. Or they might be caused by gigantic, opaque fog banks. Or both, producing a perfect storm of darkness.

But the truth is, scientists just don't know. For now, this mysterious phenomenon has them all completely in the dark.

REFLECTION

In physics, one learns that darkness *per se* doesn't really exist. Darkness is merely the absence of light. Light is what's real.

The same is true of temperature. Cold *per se* doesn't really exist. Cold is merely the absence of heat. Heat is what's real.

It's helpful to keep that in mind whenever darkness comes down on you suddenly and oppressively. First, tell yourself over and over: Darkness is not real; it's simply the absence of light. Then ask yourself over and over: What's my *main source* of light?

Is it your material success and possessions? Your perceived power and fame? Your friends and family?

If so, consider this: Material success, worldly power, friends, and even beloved family members are all subject to sudden blackouts. They can all be snuffed out in the blink of an eye, extinguishing all the light in your life and plunging you into terrifying darkness.

According to the Bible, God is the only inextinguishable light that exists in and beyond the universe. When all else goes dark in your life, cry out to him, and he—the very *creator of light*—will respond. Like the emergency-path lighting inside a commercial airplane, he will guide you—step by step—out of your present darkness and into the light.

A light that will never fail you.

THE CREATOR SPEAKS

Here on earth you will have many trials and sorrows.
But take heart, because I have overcome the world.
JOHN 16:33

Two Heads Are Better than One

Few sights are as magical as a vast meadow twinkling with fireflies on a summer evening. And few creatures are as enchanting as the tiny, fairy-like insects creating the spectacle. There are more than 2,000 species of fireflies. In North America, the Big Dipper firefly (*Photinus pyralis*) is most likely the species lighting up your backyard.

Oddly enough, a firefly is not actually a fly; it's a winged beetle. And its fiery light—usually blue-green, yellow, or red-orange—isn't hot, it's ice cold, emitted by special cells in the abdomen that combine oxygen and a bioluminescent chemical called luciferin.

Like most insects, a firefly goes through four distinct stages of life. Males start as eggs, then morph into worms—often called glowworms. Next, they go through a pupal stage before emerging as the aerial creatures that brighten our summer nights. Females pass through the same four stages, but not all of them develop wings. Instead, they remain as glowworms.

When the time comes to find a mate and procreate—the glittering finale of a firefly's multistage life—males wait until it's dark outside. Then they begin to fly around and strut their stuff.

A male in full flight will repeatedly switch its bioluminescent belly on and off (in a way that science still doesn't fully understand) in a Morse code–like pattern unique to his species—a love letter written in flashing lights. For instance, the males of a certain Texas-based species (*Photinus consisus*) blink on and off roughly every two seconds.

Meanwhile the females watch intently from nearby foliage. When a female spots her species' code in a way that strikes her fancy, she signals back the male. The two then mate and produce a wealth of eggs.

Romantic as it seems, however, this starry-eyed mating ritual isn't without its dangers. During mating season, female Pennsylvania fireflies

(*Photuris pensylvanica*) will mimic the Big Dipper's courtship code, luring unsuspecting males. As soon as a suitor cozies up to her, the female kills him, drinks his blood, and devours his organs.

REFLECTION

In a sense, life is one long, drawn-out, extravagant mating ritual. Whether it's trying to find the right spouse, the right school, or the right job, most people are trying to impress others to get something they want.

There may be times when everything seems to be playing out exactly as you'd hoped. In your quest for a mate, a very special person might say and do all the right things, leading you to believe an engagement is imminent.

In your pursuit of a top college, the admissions officer might appear to be signaling that everything is looking good—that your grades, test scores, and recommendations are amazing—leading you to start packing your bags.

In your search for your dream job, the HR director at a distinguished firm might say your application looks strong, leading you to believe you're a shoo-in.

But then everything falls apart, and you end up disappointed. Like a male Big Dipper firefly, you realize too late that you've misread the signals—or maybe the signals themselves were misleading.

Fortunately, though, you're not a firefly; you're a beloved child of God with access to his wise counsel, the Bible. When you're trying to interpret the signs about an important matter, the Bible says don't go it alone. Instead, consult friends and family, to benefit from their wisdom and insight. Above all, by taking it to God in prayer, you greatly reduce the chances of being lured into a decision that has devastating consequences.

THE CREATOR SPEAKS

Without wise leadership, a nation falls;
*   there is safety in having many advisers.*
PROVERBS 11:14

Slow and Powerful

From the time of the first explorers and geographers until recently, the consensus was that the continents have never changed shape or position and that the modern globe shows how the land has always been. In 1912, however, a German geophysicist named Alfred Wegener dared to challenge the age-old dogma.

He proposed that the continents actually slide around ever so slowly across the face of the planet and that once upon a time there was just one big supercontinent, which Wegener called Pangaea, surrounded by one big super-ocean he called Panthalassa.

Wegener claimed that Pangaea eventually broke apart, its fragments drifting away at a speed imperceptible to our human senses. What we see today, he said, is the result of that slow, inexorable dispersal.

Wegener's scientific peers fiercely rejected his hypothesis. For one thing, they couldn't imagine any natural process powerful enough to drive the movement of such enormous land masses. The Asian continent alone weighs a whopping 3,358,000,000,000,000,000,000 pounds!

By the 1960s, however, scientists admitted their error and cried uncle. They realized that the continents slip and slide atop constantly moving, subterranean molten rock, like rafts on a river. This happens at the very slow rate of one to ten centimeters per year—about the rate your fingernails grow.

Wegener's idea is now the scientific consensus, the foundation of the modern discipline of *plate tectonics*. Sadly, Wegener himself didn't live long enough to see his beliefs accepted; instead, the maverick scientist died unvindicated in 1930.

REFLECTION

Are there times you feel weighed down by a massive, continent-sized crisis that seems impossible to budge? Perhaps it's a mountain of debt. Or a nightmarish personal or professional relationship. Or a life-threatening diagnosis.

God wants to help you. But you can't just passively believe in his willingness and ability to do so. You must actively trust that he *will* help you.

This means being patient, which is tough to do in our day and age of immediate gratification—of overnight delivery, video on demand, and instant credit.

In contrast to all that, God's assistance can seem to take an eternity. Why does he act with such continental-drift-like slowness?

Why your impatience?

You see, while you're waiting impatiently for God's help, he is waiting patiently for you to be at exactly the right place at the right time for his help to produce the perfect results.

THE CREATOR SPEAKS

Wait patiently for the LORD.
> Be brave and courageous.
> Yes, wait patiently for the LORD.

PSALM 27:14

A Keen Sense of Smell

The typical dog has several hundred million smell receptors, whereas a human has only six million. What's more, a dog's olfactory bulb—the part of the brain that processes smells—is *forty times larger* than a human's.

A dog's nose is so keen it can smell when a person with epilepsy is about to have a seizure or a diabetic's sugar level is plummeting. Italian researchers trained German shepherds to detect prostate cancer with 90 percent accuracy, which beats the usual PSA (prostate specific antigen) blood test used by the medical establishment.

Dogs can also detect Parkinson's disease with 90 percent accuracy, simply by smelling a patient's T-shirt. That's remarkable given that (as of this writing) modern medicine has yet to come up with a standardized screening tool of its own for Parkinson's.

In England, Labrador retrievers can identify children with asymptomatic malaria simply by sniffing their socks.

In British Columbia, an English springer spaniel at the Vancouver General Hospital has been trained to sniff out *Clostridium difficile*, a highly contagious bacterium that causes severe diarrhea and colitis.

More recently, dogs have been trained to diagnose people with COVID-19 just by sniffing their sweat. In controlled experiments, the dogs scored a 97 percent accuracy rate, which is equal to or better than many standard PCR (polymerase chain reaction) tests.

REFLECTION

The Bible speaks of God's sense of smell—which is far more powerful and profound than even a dog's.

The Old Testament describes religious sacrifices whose aromas are pleasing to God. According to the New Testament, God finds his own smell the most pleasing of all (2 Corinthians 2:15-16). For that reason, he rejoices in the aroma of true believers, people who seek to be like him.

You, your thoughts, emotions, and behavior give off various telltale odors that only God can smell. From their redolence God can diagnose the condition of your heart, mind, soul, and spirit. With a single whiff, God can tell whether your innermost self is healthy or diseased.

But here's the good news: If you smell putrid to God, he won't rebuff you, the way *you* would anyone who smells bad. Instead, God will reach out his loving, forgiving arms and offer you a way to wash away the stink. Permanently.

THE CREATOR SPEAKS

For we [believers] are to God the pleasing aroma of Christ.
2 CORINTHIANS 2:15, NIV

High and Mighty

Dragonflies (order Odonata; suborder Anisoptera), predatory insects extraordinaire, are arguably the most effective hunters on the planet. According to a 2012 Harvard study, dragonflies successfully nail their prey about 90 percent of the time.[1] By comparison, legendary hunters such as eagles, hawks, and owls rarely achieve a success rate of more than 25 percent.

What's the secret of the dragonflies' stunning success? The unparalleled ability they have to control where they're going, even at top speed.

Most winged insects have wings that flap sloppily. That's because their wings are controlled not by muscles, but by rapid-fire deformations of their bodies—something akin to trying to clap your hands by shaking your torso.

Dragonflies have four wings, each of which is flapped and rotated by a powerful, precision muscle. This allows the insect to pull off some extremely complex, showy aerial movements that even the iconic Blue Angels can't match.

Counter stroking is when a dragonfly's hindwings and forewings flap out of sync by a full 180 degrees. This allows the insect to rise straight up like a helicopter, or to hover while moving forward in short, slow bursts.

Phased stroking is when the hindwings and forewings flap out of sync by only ninety degrees. This creates a thrust so powerful it propels a dragonfly up to thirty miles per hour, making it the fastest flying insect on earth.

Dragonflies can even fly backwards, an extremely rare ability that only hummingbirds and some flies can pull off. Best of all, dragonflies use their amazing, aerobatic arsenal to zero in and gobble up many of the insects we dislike the most, including flies, midges, and mosquitos.

REFLECTION

During those times in life when you're flying high—when things are going so well, you become intoxicated with yourself and your success— you are in grave danger of being more like a hapless flying insect than a dragonfly. You're in the greatest danger of crashing and burning.

It's a form of DUI that fells even the highest and mightiest among us. It's a perilous condition caused by *arrogance*.

The Old Testament recounts the story of Saul, whom God hand-picked and anointed to be Israel's first king. During his reign, Saul repeatedly disobeyed God, always believing that he, Saul, knew best.

Saul grew so big in his own eyes, the Bible reports, that he "went to the town of Carmel to set up a monument to himself." Disgusted with Saul's willful arrogance, God instructed the great prophet Samuel to find, anoint, and groom Saul's successor: a humble shepherd boy named David.

How high and mighty are you flying these days? How big are you in your own eyes? Are you like Saul . . . or more like David?

THE CREATOR SPEAKS

Pride goes before destruction,
*   and haughtiness before a fall.*
Better to live humbly with the poor
*   than to share plunder with the proud.*
PROVERBS 16:18-19

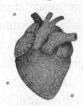

Thirst No More

In our search for extraterrestrial life, we always get excited when we find water—whether it's on a planet, moon, asteroid, or out in deep space. It's an article of faith among scientists that where there's water there can be life (see Invitation 50).

The reason for this conviction is rooted quite simply in what we see here on Earth. In one way or another, every single organism on our little blue planet relies on water.

Indeed, Earth is *saturated* with water and life. If you search hard enough and dig deep enough, even in the driest, most hostile places, you'll find H_2O and the life-forms that go with it.

Typical of all terrestrial life, the human body is mostly made of water—on average, 60 percent. That means an adult weighing 170 pounds contains about 12.2 gallons of water.

Moreover, the water in everyone's body—including yours—is ancient. That's because, roughly speaking, Earth is what we call a *closed system*, a self-contained entity. Aside from (1) constantly gaining a little mass from a smattering of meteors and comets, and (2) leaking a little air and moisture from the very top of the atmosphere (most of which is held captive by Earth's gravity), every bit of material on our planet right now has been here since day one.

Everything—including Earth's water—just keeps getting recycled and repurposed, over and over again. It means that at least some of the H_2O molecules in your body right now were inside the bodies of countless other people—many of them famous, no doubt—who have long since died and dried up.

And speaking of drying up, to prevent that from happening to you while you're still alive, you need to drink an average of four to six cups of water every day. You can survive for weeks, even months, without food; but without water, you can survive only two to four days.

REFLECTION

The Bible makes many, many references to water, both natural and spiritual.

It speaks about Jesus, the Good Shepherd, leading us to lie down by calm waters. It's a word picture of the supernatural peace God offers us amidst the Sturm und Drang of everyday life.

It also speaks about the Water of Life, the spiritual fluid you need to stay fully alive, not just here on Earth, but beyond the grave.

Earth is a paradise overflowing with natural water, but it's a desert when it comes to Living Water. The only source of that is God.

If you're sincerely interested in finding this supernatural fountain of youth, the map to it is in the Bible. God is ready, willing, and able to personally lead you to it right now.

But take note. Though he'll lead you to the source of Living Water, he will never force you to drink from it.

That's your decision to make.

THE CREATOR SPEAKS

Jesus replied, . . . "Those who drink the water I give will never be thirsty again. It becomes a fresh, bubbling spring within them, giving them eternal life."
JOHN 4:13-14

Busting through Barriers

It's easy to think of solid objects as being absolutely impenetrable. They aren't.

A clay brick is made of atoms; but about 25 percent of the brick has no atoms; it's empty space. Also, each atom itself is 99.999 percent empty space.

Moreover—and here things get really strange—according to quantum mechanics, subatomic particles—for example, an electron—are ghostly and can easily pass through solid barriers. The phenomenon is called *quantum tunneling*, but the name is misleading.

The subatomic particle doesn't actually *tunnel* through a barrier, like a drill or hungry termite. Instead, it appears to *seep* through the wall, the way we think of a specter seeping, or passing, through a solid barrier.

How is this possible? According to quantum mechanics, a subatomic particle can be in many places at once. Even if it appears to be trapped inside a box, it can also be outside the box at the same time. That's what gives the impression that it seeps through the box; in fact, it's always been outside the box to some degree.

Quantum tunneling isn't just a weird, subatomic phenomenon. Computer flash drives and many superconducting magnetic detectors, including ones used for medical diagnosis, work because of quantum tunneling. Scanning tunneling microscopes, which have enormous magnifying power, also depend on quantum tunneling.

Believe it or not, even your very own nose uses quantum tunneling to distinguish different smells.

REFLECTION

There are times in life when it feels as though we smack into a solid, brick wall. One minute we're zipping along, admiring the scenery, then suddenly—*whack!*—something happens that stops us dead in our tracks.

Maybe you've hit the proverbial glass ceiling at work. Maybe you've reached an impasse with your significant other. Or maybe you've given up on a lifelong dream.

Don't give up!

Rarely is a brick wall as solid and impenetrable as it seems. Turn to God—literally, cry out to him—and he will help you tunnel through whatever or whoever is standing in your way.

Think of God as a barrier buster, and give him a chance to prove it to you.

THE CREATOR SPEAKS

> O Sovereign LORD! You made the heavens and earth by your strong hand and powerful arm. Nothing is too hard for you!
> JEREMIAH 32:17

Electrifying Genius

There are 470 different species of stingray, but one of them is especially remarkable: the roughly one-foot-long, reddish-brown, blue-spotted common torpedo (*Torpedo torpedo*). Found primarily in the eastern Atlantic Ocean and Mediterranean Sea, the torpedo is a study in electrifying brilliance.

For starters, the platter-shaped fish has two natural kidney-shaped batteries situated on opposite sides of its broad, flat-nosed head. Made of stacked, gelatin-filled disks called *electroplaques*, the batteries combined can deliver a stunning 220-volt jolt—just like a European wall outlet.

The torpedo uses this special ability to hunt for and capture food. Buried in the ocean's sandy bottom, a hungry torpedo will generate an electric field all around itself, much as a spider spins a web.

When an unsuspecting fish swims through the invisible field—for example, a herring, porgy, or jack mackerel—the torpedo senses the disruption and pounces. In the blink of an eye, the torpedo disables its victim with a blast of electricity, then swallows it whole.

Fortunately for us, the shock from a torpedo's batteries isn't strong enough to kill a human, but it's definitely painful enough to make you want to stay away.

REFLECTION

It took the most brilliant human minds many centuries of intentional effort to *invent* electricity. It wasn't until 1800—historically speaking, like yesterday—that Italian physicist Alessandro Volta built the world's first true battery.

We congratulate ourselves for the clever invention; yet the common torpedo's batteries existed long, long before Volta's brainchild. And their compact, elegant, power-packed design puts to shame Volta's clunky, weak, unreliable batteries.

Likewise, it took us a very, very long time to invent electric field detectors—akin to the magnetic, walk-through security devices widely used in airports today. Yet, long before we ever conceived them, the torpedo already had the uncanny ability to hunt for food by detecting tiny disruptions to its body's electric field—as little as 0.01 microvolts, which is 150 million times *tinier* than the voltage of a AAA battery!

So, what do you believe? Is the common torpedo the astonishing result of a long, randomly ordered string of natural accidents? Or the intentional brainchild of a truly, brilliant inventor?

THE CREATOR SPEAKS

> *Who is this that questions my wisdom*
>   *with such ignorant words? . . .*
> *Where were you when I laid the foundations of the earth?*
>   *Tell me, if you know so much. . . .*
> *You are God's critic, but do you have the answers?*
> JOB 38:2, 4; 40:2

Beloved Outcast

In 2006, members of the International Astronomical Union (IAU) voted to remove Pluto from the official roster of our solar system's planets. The controversial decision stunned the world because the remote little planet—the runt of the litter, to be sure—had been adored by young and old alike since its discovery in 1930.

How did Pluto come to be downgraded? On the final day of the IAU's annual assembly, a group of astronomers proposed a resolution to redefine what constitutes a planet—a move clearly designed to exclude Pluto. Only a small minority of the IAU's large membership was still present, yet they managed to pass the resolution.

Presumably to minimize the predictable backlash, the same minority voted to create a new class of objects, called "dwarf planets," which fit Pluto to a tee.

The controversy still has not subsided. In fact, it has heated up in recent years with the discovery by the *New Horizons* spacecraft that Pluto is one of the most spectacular worlds in our solar system. It even seems to have key assets amenable to life, such as water and organic chemicals. Some researchers are calling for the IAU to reclassify Pluto—again—as a planet.

Arguing that an object should be considered a planet based on its attributes rather than its orbit, planetary astronomer Philip Metzger says of Pluto, "It's more dynamic and alive than Mars. The only [other] planet that has more complex geology is the Earth."[1]

REFLECTION

Do you feel small and marginalized—as if, in the grand scheme of things you don't matter? Have you been booted from—"canceled" by—social media or polite society? Have you been evicted from your house, your job, or the fellowship of your close friends?

Take heart, my friend. As the Bible explains, God delights in choosing the smallest and least among us to accomplish his grandest purposes.

He chose Abraham—an old, childless man living in the middle of nowhere—to become the patriarch of a chosen people as numerous as the stars.

He chose Moses—a reclusive, stuttering fugitive from the law—to liberate the chosen people from Egyptian slavery.

He chose Rahab—a lowly prostitute *and* Canaanite—to be an ancestor of Jesus, the Savior of the world.

So, be encouraged!

The world might be doing its best to make you feel unimportant; but to God you are invaluable, a crucial part of his cosmic-sized plans.

THE CREATOR SPEAKS

What the world thinks is worthless, useless, and nothing at all is what God has used to destroy what the world considers important.

1 CORINTHIANS 1:28, CEV

Unplumbed Depths

Deep beneath south-central Kentucky is the world's longest cave system, appropriately named Mammoth Cave National Park. With its many miles of subterranean tunnels, pits, and caverns, it is larger than the world's next two biggest cave systems combined.

Mammoth is famous for its long, tube-shaped corridors that we believe were carved by underground rivers that have since subsided. Explorers have christened these corridors with names such as Boone Avenue, Cleveland Avenue, and Kentucky Avenue.

Mammoth Cave is an example of what we call a *solution cave*. Such caves are gradually eaten out of subterranean limestone rock by an acidic solution of rainwater and carbon dioxide, which the rainwater absorbs from the air and soil it traverses.

American explorers discovered Mammoth in the late 1700s, after which many enslaved men became particularly well acquainted with its labyrinthian twists and turns while mining saltpeter there. In fact, nineteenth-century slaves are credited with mapping many of Mammoth's corridors and for guiding visitors through them.

But long before all that—roughly four thousand years ago—Native Americans knew all about Mammoth. In its seemingly endless chambers, we've discovered their footprints, bits of their clothing, remnants of the torches they used to navigate the cave, and even the perfectly mummified body of one native who was crushed beneath a huge rock while mining the cave's ubiquitous gypsum crystals.

But even long before Native Americans existed, the native wildlife knew all about Mammoth. Today, it is home to 130 species of animals and insects, some of which are unique to the cave—for instance, the eyeless Kentucky cave shrimp (*Palaemonias ganteri*). It doesn't have eyes, because none are needed in the absolute, eternal blackness of Mammoth's vast, underground realm.

To date we've carefully mapped out more than four hundred miles of the sprawling cave system. But some experts believe there are still hundreds of miles more waiting to be plumbed.

REFLECTION

According to the Bible's description of God, he is vast—far more so than Mammoth Cave. In fact, God is even bigger than infinity (see Invitation 99).

On a practical level, that means, among other things, that you and I will never fully comprehend him—physically, intellectually, or emotionally. It's a huge mistake, therefore, to second-guess God.

Yet many people do just that. All the time.

You often hear them complain, "*If* there's a God, then how come . . . ?"

What they're really saying is, "If *I* were God, then things would be different."

But you and I are not God, so we'll never know what it's like to be him. To claim otherwise—to boast, "If I were God, then things would be different"—is delusional, never mind blasphemous.

According to the Bible, you are able to have a close, personal relationship with the bigger-than-infinite creator of the universe. But don't let that go to your head. Always remember your place. He is God; you are not.

Even after a lifetime of studying the nuances of God's words and exploring his natural creation; even after staying constantly in touch with him through prayer; even after putting him first all your life—you will have plumbed only the tiniest portion of God's immeasurable being.

THE CREATOR SPEAKS

Oh, how great are God's riches and wisdom and knowledge! How impossible it is for us to understand his decisions and his ways! For who can know the LORD's thoughts? Who knows enough to give him advice?
ROMANS 11:33-34

Human Folly

Hurricanes are deadly for many reasons. They begin without warning, their trajectories are difficult to predict, and their winds and rainfall are dangerously powerful.

There's another reason hurricanes are deadly: *human folly*. People build their houses along shorelines routinely battered by hurricanes. They don't evacuate when told to do so. They brazenly walk out to the end of a pier where a hurricane is forecast to hit and party while waiting for it to arrive.

Atlantic hurricanes usually start when the air pressure off the coast of northwest Africa dips ever so slightly. Fueled by the warm tropical water, the tiny disturbance intensifies as it races across the southern Atlantic,[1] oftentimes swelling into a full-fledged hurricane.[2]

Every year, hurricanes slamming into the United States cause enormous death and destruction. In 2005, Hurricane Katrina alone claimed twelve hundred lives and caused $108 billion in damage.

These calamities are made worse by the many people who do not fear—who do not respect—the awesome power of hurricanes. Were they to do so, the death and destruction caused by these fierce storms would be greatly reduced.

REFLECTION

Who or what do you fear in life?

If, first and foremost, you don't fear God, then you are like the foolish people who build their homes along well-known hurricane pathways. Or who stubbornly refuse to evacuate when told to do so. Or who party in the face of imminent disaster.

Fearing God doesn't mean cowering in his presence. It means *acknowledging*, *respecting*, and *taking seriously* God's existence and sovereignty.

It means knowing he is mightier than any hurricane. Above all, when faced with any storm, it means going to him for perfect, hurricane-proof shelter.

THE CREATOR SPEAKS

Fear of the LORD is the foundation of wisdom.
Knowledge of the Holy One results in good judgment.
PROVERBS 9:10

Roots

The largest living organism on the planet is not what you might think. It's not the elephant or the blue whale, both of which are indeed huge; it's a 106-acre stand of quaking aspen trees in south-central Utah.

The name of this massive organism is Pando. In Latin it means "I spread."

Pando consists of forty-seven thousand individual trees. But they're counted as a single organism because they're genetically identical clones of a parent tree that began growing some eleven thousand years ago. All together this so-called "forest of one tree" weighs a whopping thirteen million pounds.

Peter Wohlleben, a German forester and author of the best-selling book *The Hidden Life of Trees*, explains how quaking aspens got their name and why they spread so efficiently: "Their leaves hang from flexible stems and flutter in the breeze, exposing first their upper and then their lower surfaces to the sun. This means both sides of the leaf can photosynthesize. This is in contrast to other species, where the underside is reserved for breathing. Thus, quaking aspens can generate more energy, and grow faster."[1]

Like all stands of quaking aspens, Pando began life as a fuzzy-covered seed, blown in the wind, that fell to the ground and took root. The seed grew up to become a single parent tree. Beneath the surface, its roots then spread far and wide. Year after year those roots sprouted new baby trees, called suckers, which eventually produced the Pando we see today.

Sadly, Pando is now struggling. Mule deer, human construction—campgrounds, cabins, houses—and fire prevention mandates are conspiring to weaken and slowly destroy Pando's development. Deer eat Pando's suckers as soon as they sprout; developers cut Pando's mature trees down for space; and Smokey Bear keeps fires from clearing away land and making room for Pando to keep expanding.

REFLECTION

Outwardly, you are just one person of eight billion on planet Earth. But in reality you and everyone else are identical: We're all made in the image of God.

The Reverend Martin Luther King Jr. put it beautifully:

> We must never forget . . . there are no gradations in the image of God. Every man from a treble-white to a bass-black is significant on God's keyboard precisely because every man is made in the image of God. One day we will learn that. We will know one day that God made us to live together as brothers and to respect the dignity and worth of every man.[2]

In a manner of speaking, we're all like a sprawling, planetwide, human Pando. We seem to be individuals, each standing on our own. But in reality, like the trees of Pando, our lives, our fates, are all connected.

Whether you—one of the eight billion human "trees" on Earth—thrive or wither and die depends on whether you are rooted in truth . . . or in sin. Moreover, your choice affects not just you, but the spiritual health of the entire organism of humanity.

THE CREATOR SPEAKS

> *The human body has many parts, but the many parts make up one whole body. . . . If one part suffers, all the parts suffer with it, and if one part is honored, all the parts are glad.*
>
> 1 CORINTHIANS 12:12, 26

Divine Creations

The North American beaver (*Castor canadensis*) and Eurasian beaver (*Castor fiber*) exemplify what scientists call *keystone species*, organisms that are relatively small in size and number but that have an outsized effect on their environment. In the case of beavers, they are like bulls in a china shop.

In Alberta, Canada, for instance, the squat, flat-tailed rodents built a dam more than 2,700 feet long by taking down thousands of trees. Visible from outer space, it is to date the world's longest beaver dam.

Typically it all begins when beavers move into a wooded area by a stream or river. They topple trees along the shoreline by chewing through the trunks with big, strong, chainsaw-like buckteeth. Each tree topples directly into the water, sparing the busy beavers the time and trouble of hauling it across land.

The beavers feed on the bark, then set about using what's left to create a dam that produces the largest possible pond.

They do this by first deftly laying down the largest tree parts *along the direction of the water's flow*, then weaving in and around them the more supple branches and twigs. They finish up by filling all the gaps with mud, stones, plants, and grass. The result is a sturdy, impregnable dam.

Just like that, the once-wooded stream or river is magically transformed into a vast, treeless wetland, an ecosystem that attracts a wide variety of new plants and animals such as frogs, turtles, geese, ducks, dragonflies, snails, mussels, worms, and various flies. Even salmon and trout use beaver ponds to spawn and overwinter.

REFLECTION

We humans, even more so than beavers, can radically transform whatever location we move into.

Sadly, all too often our efforts end up destroying more than creating, greatly spoiling the native beauty of an area. As singer Joni Mitchell so eloquently puts it: "They paved paradise and put up a parking lot."[1]

Sometimes, however, our efforts create more than they destroy, transforming something homely into something truly beautiful. Leonardo da Vinci transformed canvas and paints made from unremarkable, earthly raw materials into artwork that is indisputably heavenly.

God alone, however, can create something without destroying anything whatsoever; he alone is able to create something from nothing. As the Bible puts it, "The earth was formless and empty, and darkness covered the deep waters. . . . Then God said, 'Let there be light,' and there was light."[2]

When you set out to create something, try to do it in the least destructive way. Do it in a godly way that results in a home, neighborhood, or workplace that's far more beautiful than when you showed up with your bright ideas and ambitious plans.

THE CREATOR SPEAKS

Anyone who builds . . . may use a variety of materials—gold, silver, jewels, wood, hay, or straw. But on the judgment day, fire will reveal what kind of work each builder has done. The fire will show if a person's work has any value.

1 CORINTHIANS 3:12-13

Pay careful attention to your own work, for then you will get the satisfaction of a job well done, and you won't need to compare yourself to anyone else. For we are each responsible for our own conduct.

GALATIANS 6:4-5

A Bow of Many Colors

Over the years, scientists have learned it takes three criteria—three laws of the universe—to produce a rainbow. Absent any one of them, you get nothing.

First, the *law of refraction*. When sunlight enters an airborne water droplet, its trajectory bends inward slightly, like a dogleg.

Second, the *law of total internal reflection*. When the bent sunlight reaches the backside of the water droplet, it is reflected. Oddly, in other words, the back surface of the water droplet—though transparent to the eye—acts like a mirror.

Third, the *law of dispersion*. The bent, internally reflected sunlight exits the droplet's front surface, whereupon it fans out into all the colors of the rainbow, in this exact order: red, orange, yellow, green, blue, indigo, and violet.

Of course, this three-step process works only if sunlight *and* airborne water droplets exist at the same time—which happens only during a very narrow, very precise window of time, namely when a rainstorm (airborne water droplets) is just letting up and the sky is just beginning to clear (sunlight).

Only when *all* of the above preconditions are satisfied does a magnificent bow of many colors suddenly sweep across the sky. Scientifically speaking, it's a sign of optimism (better weather ahead), enormous beauty, and the exquisite inner workings of the cosmos.

REFLECTION

Any parent knows how painful it can be to discipline a misbehaving child. God is no different.

Time and again, throughout human history, God has had to punish us for our rebellious and wicked behavior. Each time, he was left bereaved.

For example, he flooded the earth to wipe it clean of our wanton depravity. Afterward, he promised Noah he would never do that again.

According to the Bible, God selected rainbows to be the universal reminders of that promise, a sign specifically designed to appear after thunderstorms, just when the clouds are parting and the sun is coming out again.

THE CREATOR SPEAKS

I have placed my rainbow in the clouds. It is the sign of my covenant with you and with all the earth.... Never again will the floodwaters destroy all life.

GENESIS 9:13, 15

The Walking Dead

The jewel wasp (*Ampulex compressa*) has an inch-long, iridescent blue-green body and bright red legs that make it sparkle like a gorgeous gemstone. In truth, however, it's a horrifying predator.

When a female jewel wasp is ready to lay her eggs, she searches out a cockroach, which is quite often four to five times her size. Sneaking up on the unsuspecting roach, she stings it with a toxin that instantly paralyzes its front legs, so it can't scurry away.

The jewel wasp then stings the cockroach's brain in two places, using special sensors to zap the targets with laser-like precision. The two stings turn the cockroach into a full-blown zombie.

Though still alive, the vegetated victim has no desire or ability to flee from the female wasp. It simply lolls around, compulsively cleaning itself.

The jewel wasp then goes off to search for a burrow. Once found, she returns to the living-dead cockroach, breaks off one of its antennae and tastes its blood.

Reassured that all is now set for the grand finale, the jewel wasp grabs hold of the zombie's remaining antenna and guides it back to her burrow. There the wasp lays a single egg inside the zombie's body before entombing it with twigs and rocks.

Several days later, the wasp larva hatches and instantly begins feasting on the zombified cockroach's body, everything except its outer shell. The voracious young jewel wasp takes a whole month to finish its meal, after which it climbs out of the burrow, finds a mate, and proceeds to perpetuate its gruesome life cycle.

REFLECTION

According to the Bible, there are entities called demons that can enslave us, just as jewel wasps enslave cockroaches. Even if you find it hard to believe in actual demons, there's no denying that everyone—including you—can fall prey to everyday temptations that have demon-like effects.

Vices such as pride, lust, envy, selfishness, and rebellion can sting you, quickly turning you into a zombie. Like one of those poor, wretched cockroaches, you find yourself doing (and saying) things you normally wouldn't.

Deep down inside, you might be aware of what's happening to you, yet you feel helpless to fight it. But are you really? Are you truly, completely helpless against demon-like vices?

No.

You're not a cockroach. You're a human being, made in the image of God. As such, you possess a supernatural power that can stand up to the stings of the spirit world's marauding jewel wasps. The Bible calls this superpower God's Spirit.

It's not an easy thing to fully understand. But one aspect is quite clear: God's Spirit alone has the ability to make the walking dead . . . live again.

THE CREATOR SPEAKS

Letting your sinful nature control your mind leads to death. But letting the Spirit control your mind leads to life and peace.
ROMANS 8:6

Size Isn't Everything

Adélie penguins (*Pygoscelis adeliae*) are small, adorable-looking creatures that live, hunt, and breed in the Antarctic. On average, a full-grown Adélie weighs no more than ten pounds and stands barely two feet high.

But the Adélies' modest physical stature belies their enormously courageous personality. So little scares these bold, diminutive amphibious birds that they actually go looking for trouble.

The early twentieth-century British explorer Robert Falcon Scott left behind reports of the Adélies' astonishing, derring-do behavior. For instance, the penguins routinely confronted Scott's barking, howling, snarling pack of sled dogs. Whenever Scott's men tried shooing the penguins away—worried for their safety—the fearless Adélies pecked and slapped the men and pressed ahead with their confrontation.

A BBC cameraman filmed an incident that epitomizes the breathtaking bravery of Adélie penguins. It happened when a small group of emperor penguin chicks became separated from the main pack.

As their name implies, emperors are the largest of all penguin species. Adults weigh in at nearly one hundred pounds and stand nearly four feet high—about ten times the size of the average adult Adélie.

In the incident recorded by the BBC, the emperor chicks suddenly found themselves in the crosshairs of an Antarctic petrel (*Thalassoica antarctica*) looking for a meal. The hungry bird—a fierce, agile predator sporting a three-foot-plus wingspan—had the ability to dive-bomb the chicks with lightning speed.

Just when things looked bleak for the emperor chicks, a solo Adélie penguin showed up out of nowhere and waddled purposefully to the rescue. The Adélie was smaller than the chicks and the ravenous, winged predator; but the pint-sized penguin's daring attitude was so intimidating, the petrel quickly wheeled around and flew away.[1]

And the drama didn't stop there. Turning his attention on the terror-stricken chicks, the little hero gathered them together and shepherded them safely all the way back to their pack.

REFLECTION

The Bible candidly warns us that we will face trials and tribulations in this world—in some cases, terrifying ones that seem insurmountable. However, it also tells us to take heart, to be brave, because God is always ready to rescue us. We only need to ask for his help.

The Old and New Testaments are filled with inspiring reports of this supernatural promise being fulfilled. David facing Goliath. Moses facing the Red Sea. Martha and Mary facing the death of their brother, Lazarus.

In each case, God emboldened people who felt small and afraid. He transformed them into fearless little Adélies, who then rose up and overcame their big, scary challenges.

Perhaps at this very minute you are doing battle with a terrifying, seemingly insurmountable behemoth. Don't be cowed by it, no matter how petrifying it might seem.

Instead, call to mind the intrepid little Adélies from Antarctica. Call on the Lord, stand tall against your intimidating giant, and watch it flee.

THE CREATOR SPEAKS

My foes attack me all day long....
But when I am afraid,
    I will put my trust in you.
I praise God for what he has promised.
    I trust in God, so why should I be afraid?
PSALM 56:1, 3-4

Life Support

Your entire physical being quite *literally* hangs on your skeleton. Your bones keep you upright, well-articulated, and fully mobile—and they support and protect all your vital organs.

You're able to walk and run with elegance because a whopping one-half of all your bones—106 of 206—are dedicated solely to your hands and feet. You're able to hear a pin drop because your ears have extremely fine bones, like the one-tenth-inch-long *stirrup*, your skeleton's tiniest member. You're able to chew tough foods because of the mandible's incredible strength. And you're able to stand and walk because of the femur, your skeleton's strongest member.

We've known for some while that the insides of your bones contain sponge-like marrow, minerals, and fat, all of which help make red and white blood cells; house your all-purpose stem cells; and can help trigger your critical fight-or-flight response in times of danger.

But we now know the insides of your bones also help regulate your insulin level via a hormone called *osteocalcin*. "The discovery that our bones are responsible for regulating blood sugar in ways that were not known before completely changes our understanding of the function of the skeleton," says Dr. Gerard Karsenty, chairman of the department of genetics and development at Columbia University Medical Center.[1]

On top of all that, your skeleton constantly repairs itself, and it grows and shrinks with time. Amazingly, during the prime of your life, your skeleton completely replaces itself every ten years.

REFLECTION

Everyone has a worldview. It dictates how you *see* everything—the world, God, yourself, and others—which, in turn, dictates how you *respond* to everything.

What's more, your worldview, like your body, is supported by a skeleton. An internal structure comprising three key elements: *foundation*, *size*, and *center*.

The *foundation* of your worldview consists of all the beliefs you hold dear but can't prove to be true. Its *size* corresponds to how big you perceive reality to be. Its *center* is the one thing most important to you, the one thing for which you most devoutly take a knee.

Even if your worldview is fanciful, chances are it will carry you along—until, that is, trouble befalls you, at which time your fanciful worldview will be sorely tested.

If your worldview aligns well with absolute reality, it will stand up to the test, like a healthy skeleton. If it aligns poorly with absolute reality, your worldview will collapse like a diseased skeleton.

What's your worldview's foundation . . . size . . . and center?

Take a moment today to examine the three key members of your worldview's skeleton. It's nothing less than a matter of life and death.

THE CREATOR SPEAKS

> *Don't copy the behavior and customs of this world, but let God transform you into a new person by changing the way you think. Then you will learn to know God's will for you, which is good and pleasing and perfect.*
> ROMANS 12:2

Life Force

The earth has an absolutely amazing ability to heal itself, to bounce back from utter, seemingly irreversible devastation. Consider, for instance, the ecosystem in and around the city of Chernobyl in northern Ukraine.

In 1986, Chernobyl's nuclear reactor exploded, releasing about four hundred times more radiation than the 1945 A-bomb dropped on Hiroshima. More than a hundred thousand residents were permanently relocated, and the Chernobyl Exclusion Zone (CEZ)—some sixteen hundred square miles, or half again the size of Rhode Island—became off-limits for humans.

At first, excess radiation ravaged the area's flora and fauna. At precisely ground zero, a stand of pine trees killed in the explosion is now called the Red Forest because of the rusty hue of the dead tree bark.

Within months, however—lo and behold!—the local plants and animals began to recover. Today, scientists studying the CEZ report radiation levels that are actually lower than in many surrounding regions. *Incredible.*

Moreover, the CEZ is now teeming with wildlife. In fact, "researchers . . . spied tracks made by species including wild boar, elk, roe deer, red deer, wolf, fox, weasel, lynx, pine marten, raccoon dog, mink, ermine, stone marten, polecat, European hare, white hare, and red squirrel."[1] And there are now *seven times* more wolves in the CEZ than in nearby areas.

Ecologist Jim Beasley offers this explanation for the miraculous recovery: "We believe the high density of wolves . . . is due to a combination of abundant prey populations, greatly limited human activity, and lack of hunting pressure."[2]

Whatever the reason, it's clear that scientists in the past have grossly overestimated the long-term damaging effects of radioactive pollution and underestimated nature's phenomenal life force. Ecologists the world over are now declaring that the Chernobyl Exclusion Zone has become a veritable Garden of Eden for wildlife.

REFLECTION

Have you ever experienced a period of utter devastation in your life? Maybe you made a really bad decision, suffered a financial collapse, or received some grim news.

If you're ever in a seemingly hopeless situation, it can feel like the end of the road, like you will never be able to find happiness in life again. But here's one important truth to remember: Devastation is overrated. With God's help, not only can you survive it, but you can actually flourish in its wake, as never before.

Naturally, that's a difficult truth for many people to swallow. Their lives on this earth are all they know and hold dear; so when it all comes crashing down, it seems like the absolute end of the world.

But God operates in a much vaster reality than you and I do. As the loving author of life, he has the power and the desire to restore us from whatever devastation we suffer. We are never so far gone that God cannot return us to wholeness, in this life or the next.

THE CREATOR SPEAKS

Look, I am making everything new! . . . I am the Alpha and the Omega—the Beginning and the End. To all who are thirsty I will give freely from the springs of the water of life . . . and I will be their God, and they will be my children.

REVELATION 21:5-7

Stealthy Communication

An elephant, the largest land animal on the planet, is the only mammal that, from birth to death, never stops growing. By the time it dies, an elephant can weigh as much as 18,000 pounds and stand as high as thirteen feet.

Equally remarkable, if not more so, is an elephant's long, multipurpose trunk. Controlled by 40,000 muscles, it is strong enough to lift a 600-pound log and dexterous enough to pick up a small, flat coin.

An elephant also uses its trunk to communicate—by waving it around in distinct ways, like a sailor at sea waving semaphore flags.

An elephant also uses its trunk to trumpet various calls—like a bugler signaling a troop of cavalrymen. Scientists have identified more than seventy distinct elephant calls, many of them at frequencies far too low for the human ear to hear.

Those high-powered, low-frequency calls cause a rumbling in the ground that elephants as far as six miles away can detect through their feet. Elephants use these stealthy calls to find a mate, communicate danger, and locate the herd whenever they get separated from it.

REFLECTION
....

According to the Bible, God communicates with you in ways that your physical senses can't detect, but that your spirit can. It's akin to elephants picking up signals with their feet, not their ears.

God's messages often manifest themselves as visual impressions, feelings, or thoughts. Even when they come across as conventional audio messages, they aren't really that.

Sometimes, the communiques are completely subliminal. Without understanding why, you suddenly feel the urge to do something, go somewhere, or say something.

It takes experience to discern God's prompting, to distinguish his communications from your purely natural sensations. But with time and practice, the differences become clearer, even glaring.

So be encouraged. If you are new to the practice of listening for God's messages amid the din of today's noisy world and your heart's own desires, get to know God's ways by reading the Bible. Then silence yourself—go somewhere quiet—and patiently, humbly, listen for his still, small voice.

THE CREATOR SPEAKS

My sheep listen to my voice; I know them, and they follow me.
I give them eternal life, and they will never perish.
JOHN 10:27-28

A Fertile Life

On the Norwegian island of Spitsbergen, well above the Arctic Circle, sits a highly secured building called the Svalbard Global Seed Vault (aka the Doomsday Vault). Locked inside for safekeeping are more than one million kinds of plant seeds gathered from all over the world.

One remarkable thing about seeds is that they come in all sorts of sizes. Yet, in every case, the seed is always *minuscule* compared to the plant it becomes.

At one extreme, the world's smallest seed is said to belong to the New Caledonian orchid (*Anoectochilus imitans*), native to Fiji, New Caledonia, and Samoa. The seed is about two-thousandths of an inch (0.05 mm) across, yet it grows into a flowering plant hundreds of times bigger than that.

At the other extreme, the world's largest seed belongs to the sea coconut (*Lodoicea maldivica*), or coco de mer, which thrives on certain islands of the Seychelles in the Indian Ocean. Coco de mer seeds can be a foot across, which is impressive; but even more impressive is what they grow into: ninety-foot-tall palm trees.

Surprisingly, small seeds often outperform big seeds. Hence the saying: Don't judge a seed by its seed coat.

For instance, the seeds of a sugar pine (*Pinus lambertiana*)—native to the mountains of Oregon, California, and Western Mexico—are about 100,000 times *tinier* than giant coco de mer seeds. Yet sugar pines can grow taller than 270 feet—triple the height of typical coco de mer trees and nearly as tall as the Statue of Liberty!

REFLECTION

According to the Bible, truths are like seeds. Bury them deep in your heart, attend to them faithfully, and they will flower into many blessings.

But it's not enough just to believe that, or merely to read the Bible—even Atheists do that. You must live by the truths contained in the Bible and elsewhere or you'll never see them flower in your life.

Jesus addressed this matter with his disciples when relating the famous parable of the seeds.

Some people's hearts are like pavement, he explained, so the seeds of truth stand no chance of ever germinating. Other people's hearts are receptive, but their commitment to the seeds soon lapses, so the seeds quickly shrivel and die. Still others have hearts that nurture the seeds, but also leave room for weeds, which eventually choke out the seedlings.

Only a person who seriously seeks a close relationship with truth—and the source of truth, God himself—possesses the optimal conditions for growth. In that person's life, the seeds of truth germinate quickly, grow steadily, take root solidly, and mature fully into countless blessings not only for that person, but for the entire world.

THE CREATOR SPEAKS

Here is another illustration Jesus used: "The Kingdom of Heaven is like a mustard seed planted in a field. It is the smallest of all seeds, but it becomes the largest of garden plants; it grows into a tree, and birds come and make nests in its branches."
MATTHEW 13:31-32

Elixir of Life

Most living things on Earth can do without more than 90 percent of the 118 known chemical elements. But the one thing they absolutely *need* is liquid water. The typical human body is about 60 percent water. The average fish, 75 percent water. The average tomato, 94 percent water.

Why is water—H_2O—so critically important to all plant and animal life? Here are three reasons:

1. Water dissolves more things than anything else in the universe; that's why it's called the *great universal solvent*. It has an unrivaled ability to liquify, circulate, and deliver innumerable nutrients to the vital organs of a living body.
2. Water remains liquid over an unusually broad range of temperatures. From 32°F all the way up to 212°F.
3. Water freezes in an unusual way. Most substances—such as the air in your tires—expand when they get hot and *shrink* when they get cold. But water behaves in exactly the opposite way. It shrinks when heated and expands when cooled. That's why ice floats—it's less dense than liquid water.

    This is a very big deal, because during the winter or an ice age, lakes and oceans freeze. If water shrank when frozen, became denser and sank, bodies of water would freeze from the bottom up, eventually becoming solid ice. Aquatic life could not survive such a situation.

    Because ice floats, lakes and oceans freeze from the top down. The ice on top helps to insulate the liquid water underneath, thwarting rampant freezing and enabling life to survive.

REFLECTION

Do you believe the extraordinary properties of water are accidents of nature? If so, the Bible says you are greatly mistaken.

According to the biblical description of creation, water didn't form accidentally. It was an intentional part of God's design.

Water was present at the very beginning of time; it's an essential, life-giving material God used to shape the entire cosmos.

That's why, among other things, we find water in so many places throughout the heavens, including Mars. And why scientists hold out hope we'll find life elsewhere in the universe.

THE CREATOR SPEAKS

The earth was formless and empty, and darkness covered the deep waters. And the Spirit of God was hovering over the surface of the waters.... Then God said, "Let the waters swarm with fish ... and every living thing that scurries and swarms in the water."

GENESIS 1:2, 20-21

Job #1

Ants, the most common insect in the world, exist on every continent except Antarctica. That's the only place they won't spoil your picnic.

Ants are famous for their strength. A mighty elephant can lift one-fifth of its body weight; but a tiny ant can lift more than five times its body weight.

Ants are equally noteworthy for their stable, sophisticated, altruistic societies. Like Alexandre Dumas' famous Three Musketeers, ants live and die by the motto: All for one, and one for all.

For instance, a single ant in trouble will call out for help by (a) releasing an alarm pheromone or (b) rubbing its legs against its abdomen, producing a plaintive squeak—akin to dialing 911. In each case, the solo ant's entire colony will spring into action and send out a rescue party.

When a foraging ant discovers food, it instantly dashes around alerting its fellow foragers by tapping on their antennae. If alone, it runs immediately to the colony, leaving behind a chemical trail its fellow ants can easily follow to the booty.

Above all, every single ant in a colony has a specific job to do. And, invariably, it performs the task with excellence.

A queen's number one job, for instance, is to lay eggs—in some cases, millions of eggs every year. Other ants have the job of removing the eggs from the queen's abdomen or licking them to keep them hydrated.

Still other ants have the job of guarding their colony's entryways or spreading out far and wide to hunt for food.

Worker ants have the job of digging their colony's many tunnels and chambers, and remarkably, they do so one bite at a time. Scientists estimate that all the worker ants in the world dig out a grand total of sixteen billion tons of dirt a year.

REFLECTION

According to the Bible, you have a God-given destiny. It's your number one job in life, and God has equipped you with a unique set of natural talents to perform it with excellence.

But beware: If you are skeptical or willful, you'll run into headwinds. Inevitably, you'll doggedly try doing things you're not well-equipped to do.

Such skepticism and willfulness lead to frustration and even depression. Peace and joy come only when you seek and find your destiny.

That's when you find your true self and the reason you exist.

THE CREATOR SPEAKS

In his grace, God has given us different gifts for doing certain things well. . . . If your gift is serving others, serve them well. If you are a teacher, teach well. If your gift is to encourage others, be encouraging. If it is giving, give generously. If God has given you leadership ability, take the responsibility seriously. And if you have a gift for showing kindness to others, do it gladly.

ROMANS 12:6-8

Let Me Count the Ways

At the beach, each grain of sand you lie on or kick around or shape into castles has a fascinating story to tell. A story about the long, long, long journey it had to take in order to land on the shoreline of a mighty ocean or lake.

A typical grain of sand—by definition, any particle 0.002 to 0.08 inches across—begins life as something much larger. A mountainous boulder, an animal bone, a seashell, a crystal, a chunk of glass, and so forth.

Over many, many years, the large object is steadily worn down by wind, rain, and other erosive forces. Bit by bit, the large object is ground down into smaller objects—technically called *gravel*—that end up being washed into a stream or river.

During the ensuing wild, watery ride, the gravel-sized objects scrape against themselves and other hard objects and are ground down to even smaller objects: *sand*. Or smaller still: *silt*. From there, they are dispersed far and wide by wind and water.

Inevitably, a grain's long voyage ends up in a desert, sandpit, beach, or any number of other resting places. Lying there by the trillions, their once-mighty stature now greatly diminished, the grains all look the same, even though they aren't.

Inspect grains of sand under a microscope and you'll see the widely different stories they have to tell. Their different colors alone—browns, blacks, greys with flairs of red, orange, blue, green, white, and purple—all speak of their sundry, far-flung provenances.

Moreover, in one of nature's great ironies, sand—despite its lowly appearance—has many very important uses. In artwork, landscaping, and children's playgrounds—and above all, in construction—sand is all-important.

REFLECTION

From God's cosmic-sized perspective, we look like grains of sand. If he were a deity who keeps his distance, we'd all look tiny and colorless.

But the God described in the Bible—the creator of the universe—long ago revealed himself to be approachable. He's a deity who values relationships, whether they be among the heavenly hosts or us earthly mortals.

God bothers to look at each of us up close, and he wishes to love each of us up close. He recognizes and glories in our differences—the better to fulfill his diverse priorities—yet values us equally.

How much does God love and cherish you? So much so, the Bible explains, that he's always thinking about you—and hoping for the same in return.

How often will you be thinking of God today?

THE CREATOR SPEAKS

How precious are your thoughts about me, O God.
They cannot be numbered!
I can't even count them;
they outnumber the grains of sand!
PSALM 139:17-18

Perfect Vision

Eagles (family Accipitridae) have the keenest vision of any vertebrate on the planet. That's because they have human-sized eyeballs with superhuman abilities. What a person with perfect vision can see at twenty feet, an eagle can see at one hundred feet.

An eagle's eyes are crammed with about five times more color receptors (*cones*) than ours: one million per square millimeter versus our 200,000. That means eagles are much better at spotting creatures camouflaged against a similar-colored background.

It also means eagles can see many more colors than we can, including trails left by animals whose urine reflects UV light, which is completely invisible to us.

Eagles also have a super-developed *fovea*, the central, most visually acute part of the retina. Scientists speculate that this superhuman fovea acts like a telephoto lens when necessary, enabling eagles to see faraway objects with astonishing clarity.

Finally, eagles have a much wider field of view than we do: a whopping 340° (out of a maximum possible 360°) versus our 180°. It means eagles can see almost everything around and behind them . . . *without rotating their heads!*

REFLECTION

The Bible describes a God who's attentive to, not aloof from, his creation. He watches us all the way from heaven with a penetrating, clear-eyed vision that puts even sharp-eyed eagles to shame.

God doesn't just look *at* you—at your choices, behavior, and outward emotions—but *through* you. His vision is so acute it perceives your innermost thoughts, motives, frustrations, hurts, and yearnings.

Because of that, God knows you better than you know yourself. He knows you *perfectly*—which is both scary and comforting.

Scary, because he sees right through your public persona and subtlest, cleverest deceptions. Comforting, because even though he sees you in the worst possible light, he still loves you and yearns to help you become the best person you can be, the person he *made* you to be.

So if you're hiding from God, please stop. Actively seek him out and start seeing in yourself what God sees in you.

THE CREATOR SPEAKS

> The LORD still rules from heaven.
> He watches everyone closely,
>   examining every person on earth.

PSALM 11:4

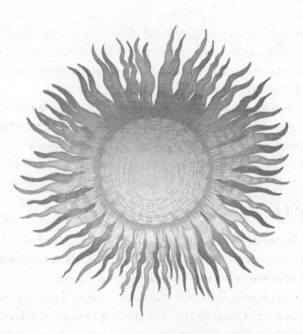

Great Expectations

Every now and then, the sky produces sudden, short-lived, deafening booms that rattle buildings—yet destroy nothing. These strange, invisible explosions, reported all over the world, are called *skyquakes*.

Witnesses liken skyquakes to thunderous cannon shots, explosions, and sonic booms. They often occur near oceans and other bodies of water, but not always.

Even though they're loud enough to wake people from a deep sleep, they're completely harmless; nothing untoward, not even so much as a flash of light, accompanies the phenomenon.

Possible explanations of them are all over the map. Perhaps skyquakes are triggered by sudden twitches of Earth's continental shelves; or by the collapse of underwater caves; or by the detonation of explosive gases escaping from underground vents.

Other possible explanations are out of this world. For example, perhaps skyquakes are caused by extra-powerful solar winds slamming into Earth's upper atmosphere.

Yet another idea is that skyquakes are caused by meteorites crashing into our atmosphere at supersonic speeds, thus setting off hair-raising sonic booms. But they also set off meteor showers—so-called shooting stars—that are bright fireworks visible from great distances, which is not the case with skyquakes.

All speculation aside, truth is, skyquakes are a bona fide mystery that our best minds haven't been able to solve.

REFLECTION

In your day-to-day life, you face truly impenetrable mysteries. No matter how smart you are, they defy understanding and make you want to pull your hair out.

Is there a best way to deal with mysteries? Yes, and it begins with *expecting* them in your life; that way, you aren't completely rattled when they happen.

Each morning when you wake up, consciously *expect* things to happen that will beggar your imagination, that will blow your mind, for better or worse. You might even go so far as to *expect* each new day to be your last day.

If that sounds morbid, think again. By living each day as if it's your last, by expecting to be slammed by life's skyquakes—sudden, inexplicable, unnerving events—you are far better prepared to handle the consequences.

You're also far less likely to take life for granted, and far more likely to appreciate life for the precious gift it is.

THE CREATOR SPEAKS

> Even when I walk
>> through the darkest valley,
> I will not be afraid,
>> for you [Lord] are close beside me.
> Your rod and your staff
>> protect and comfort me.

PSALM 23:4

Trial by Fire

The life cycle of a typical pine tree exemplifies the importance of perfect timing, plus the counterintuitive benefits of suffering. And it all begins with pinecones.

Female pinecones (*megasporangiate strobilus*) are large, woody, and usually grow on the upper branches of the tree. They contain the tree's seeds, deep within protective layers of hard, oftentimes barbed, scales.

Male pinecones (*microsporangiate strobilus*) are usually small, soft, and grow in clusters on the lower branches of the tree. They contain the pollen that fertilizes the female's seeds.

Female pinecones typically take about two years to fully develop. During this time, their scales are shut tight, even sealed with resin, to safeguard against the elements and predators.

When the female cones mature, they wait for the air temperature to be perfectly warm and nurturing. Only then do the tightly bound cones spring open, releasing their precious cache of seeds, free at last to be fertilized by the pollen from the male cones.

In some species—for example, the jack pine and lodgepole pine—the female cones open only when scorched by a hot fire. Scientists speculate this behavior gives the trees an advantage over competing species devastated by an inferno.

Because of that, our well-intentioned efforts to prevent forest fires actually thwart the natural reproduction strategy of jack pines, lodgepole pines, and other such species. That unintended consequence, in turn, hinders the proliferation of all the wildlife that depends on these fire-loving trees, such as black bears, white-tailed deer, snowshoe hares, and many kinds of songbirds.

REFLECTION

Nobody likes to suffer. Even Jesus, in the garden of Gethsemane, felt the powerful urge to avoid suffering.

Yet anguish is unavoidable. All the money in the world, the biggest house on the block, and the fanciest job title can't keep grief at bay.

But strange as it sounds, that's not entirely bad news, because suffering can have positive, unexpected consequences. By upending our comfortable lives, a tragedy can jolt us into reordering our priorities in healthier ways.

But it all depends on where God ranks on your list of priorities. If he isn't your *top* priority, you will have nowhere to turn the next time suffering comes—as it inevitably will.

God comforts, encourages, and empowers us during times of great trouble. Even more, he uses the painful experiences in our lives to bless us and others in unexpected ways.

THE CREATOR SPEAKS

I have told you all this so that you may have peace in me. Here on earth you will have many trials and sorrows. But take heart, because I have overcome the world.

JOHN 16:33

Harmony

Kelp plants, by far the most spectacular forms of marine algae, come in all shapes and sizes. The most striking kind of all is the giant kelp (*Macrocystis pyrifera*).

Giant kelp thrive in the sun-dappled coastal waters of the world's oceans, growing up to 175 feet tall! Wherever they grow in abundance, they resemble enchanted underwater forests teeming with life.

It all begins when a baby kelp anchors itself to the ocean's rocky bottom. Soon it soars upward like one of Jack's fabled beanstalks, growing up to two feet a day and sprouting pennant-shaped blades as it grows. Once it reaches the water's surface, it fans out into a massive canopy.

A full-grown kelp plant would normally collapse under its tremendous weight. But small air bladders attached to its many blades keep the plant afloat.

Giant kelp forests rank as one of the most diverse of all ocean communities, a veritable paradise for hundreds of species. The kelp itself is food for invertebrates such as snails, slugs, abalones, sea urchins, and bat stars—which, in turn, are food for critters such as crabs, rockfishes, and sea stars. Giant kelp forests also provide shelter for seals, sea lions, and gray whales—especially their young.

Before going to sleep, sea otters wrap themselves in a strong kelp blade to keep from drifting into danger during the night. Snowy egrets (*Egretta thula*) and other aquatic birds stand atop or fly over a kelp forest's canopy to feed off the insects, tiny fish, and crustaceans that swarm there.

But a kelp forest's existence is fragile. It hangs on maintaining one thing: *harmony*.

Just one seemingly small disharmony and the entire magnificent ecosystem comes crashing down. All its heavenly diversity and abundance is snuffed out.

Tragically, today we're seeing that happen before our very eyes. In many kelp forests around the world—including ones off the coast of Southern California—we've overhunted the sea otter, inadvertently triggering a catastrophic chain reaction.

Without sea otters, which eat sea urchins, the urchin population explodes. Left unchecked, sea urchins will eat an entire kelp forest to death.

The demise of a kelp forest spells doom for the myriad organisms that depend on it. All that's left is a wasteland scientists call an *urchin barren*.

REFLECTION

The Bible speaks about *the body of Christ*—the diverse, vibrant, worldwide community of Christians. A corpus of believers who proclaim, promote, and pursue God's will on earth.

Each Christian is expected to contribute his or her gifts to the whole. Each gift is unique and valuable because each believer is unique and valuable.

Some Christians are arms, others are legs. Still others are eyes and ears. As long as they function according to God's intentions, his earthly Kingdom runs true to its purpose.

But even if just one person sows disharmony or tries to be something they're not cut out to be, the entire body suffers. So, if you're a Christian, be careful not to become like a destructive sea urchin.

Your gift might not be as glamorous as you wish, but it's essential. By sharing it wisely and generously, you help keep the Christian community from becoming an urchin barren.

THE CREATOR SPEAKS

Make every effort to keep yourselves united in the Spirit, binding yourselves together with peace.
EPHESIANS 4:3

A Slow Death

According to the second law of thermodynamics, the universe is dying out. But is that really true? *Yes*, and here's how we know it:

- Heat is invariably generated by burning some kind of fuel. You, for instance, generate heat by eating.
- Heat naturally flows from hot to cold, never the other way around. It's like water, which naturally flows from high to low.
- Flows of heat keep bodies and machines alive. Stop the flows and all bodies and machines will die.
- As heat flows from hot to cold, it levels out the hot and cold regions of the universe. One day, therefore, all hot and cold regions will be wiped out and the universe will be uniformly lukewarm.
- Without any hot and cold regions, heat will stop flowing and everything—the entire cosmos—will die.

Put simply, there's an epic struggle between life and death happening throughout the universe right now, and death is gaining the upper hand everywhere. As Sigmund Freud put it, "The goal of all life is death."[1]

That is the central message of the second law of thermodynamics. It's an arresting, prophetic law of nature.

REFLECTION

In the Bible, Jesus warns his disciples: "Here on earth you will have many trials and sorrows."[2] It was his way of stating the second law of thermodynamics; of saying that we live in a sick and dying world.

But he didn't stop there. In the same verse, he goes on to deliver some good news: "Take heart, because I have overcome the world."

What exactly does he mean by *overcome*?

The answer comes when Jesus speaks to a woman named Martha, who is very upset because her brother, Lazarus, has just died. Jesus tells her that death is reversible. "I am the resurrection and the life. Anyone who believes in me will live, even after dying. . . . Do you believe this, Martha?"[3]

In the parlance of science, Jesus is saying he has the power to *overcome* the second law of thermodynamics. To *overcome* a universe where death is defeating life.

And then he proves it. First, by bringing Lazarus back to life; then, months later, by coming back to life himself.

After that, he promises to return to Earth to permanently repair our lethal universe. To breathe new life into it and thereby reverse the second law of thermodynamics—*permanently*.

THE CREATOR SPEAKS

I saw a new heaven and a new earth, for the old heaven and the old earth had disappeared. . . . And I saw the holy city, the new Jerusalem, coming down from God out of heaven. . . . I heard a loud shout from the throne, saying, ". . . There will be no more death or sorrow or crying or pain. All these things are gone forever. . . . I am making everything new!"
REVELATION 21:1-5

By Design

There are many people who sincerely believe the universe is a spectacular accident, forged blindly by natural laws that have always existed. Modern cosmologists, however, have discovered compelling evidence that the cosmos is tailor-made for life in a way that natural laws and chance alone cannot explain.

One such cosmologist is Sir Martin Rees. As of this writing, he's Great Britain's Astronomer Royal and a devout Atheist who states quite bluntly: "I've got no religious beliefs at all."

In his excellent book *Just Six Numbers: The Deep Forces That Shape the Universe*, Sir Martin lists a half-dozen numerical indicators—vital signs, if you will—that together point to one startling conclusion: The universe is built to support life not just here on planet Earth, but everywhere.

Against all odds, each vital sign has precisely the value needed for life to exist. If even one of the six vital signs were off by just a smidgen—for instance, in the case of the vital sign called Lambda, off by just one part in a trillion trillion trillion trillion trillion trillion trillion trillion trillion trillion—the cosmos would be one, cavernous ghost town.

This striking synchrony cannot easily or reasonably be chalked up to mere luck. Even if the laws of nature (never mind where they themselves came from) had billions of years to throw the dice, they still couldn't produce the six precise vital signs we see today.

That's the conclusion even Sir Martin, the committed Atheist, now supports. It's undeniable, he confesses with sublime understatement, that "we are in a privileged subset of all possible universes."[1]

REFLECTION

Despite what we now know about the aforementioned vital signs, it's still possible to dream up far-fetched ways to explain why the universe is so precisely built to support life. One such example is the multiverse hypothesis.

According to this imaginative idea, our world is just one of an *infinite number* of worlds—the one that just happened to get lucky. It's like someone winning the lottery; the odds are against it, but there's nothing mysterious or surprising about it.

This idea has been floating around for many decades now, and no one has yet come up with a way to test it. So, for now, it remains a fanciful figment of the fertile human imagination and doesn't qualify as a legitimate—that is, a testable, falsifiable—scientific hypothesis.

Other proposed concepts fall equally short of explaining why our universe is wired for life. What's more, like the multiverse idea, they all border on—if not outright fall into—the category of the supernatural.

In fact, they are all even *more* supernatural and *more* contrived than the simple, biblical explanation for the exceptionalism of our universe. After all, what's simpler than claiming that something truly extraordinary is the handiwork of a truly extraordinary creator?

THE CREATOR SPEAKS

In the beginning God created the heavens and the earth.... Then God said, "Let the waters swarm with fish and other life. Let the skies be filled with birds of every kind.... Let the earth produce every sort of animal."... Then God said, "Let us make human beings in our image, to be like us."

GENESIS 1:1, 20, 24, 26

Facing Danger

A squid looks prehistoric, with a streamlined, tubular body; a killer, parrot-like beak; eight short arms with suction cups; and two long tentacles with suction cups, teeth, and hooks. Incredibly, it can grow to be sixty-plus feet long and weigh more than a ton.

You'd think an animal so ferocious-looking would be fearless; but all squid—even the giant ones—worry constantly about predators, such as whales, sharks, albatrosses, seals, and dolphins. That's why they're equipped with some very impressive defenses.

For starters, squid are exceptional swimmers. Their tubular bodies—called mantles—act like muscular pumps, sucking seawater in from the front and squirting it out the back, propelling the squid forward at up to twenty-five miles per hour.

Squid can also escape danger by releasing clouds of a very opaque ink or, as in the case of the three-inch-long "fire shooter" squid (*Heteroteuthis dispar*), giving off a blinding cloud of bioluminescent chemicals called photophores.

Lastly, thanks to skin cells called chromatophores, squid can change color in a fraction of a second—far faster than a chameleon. This exceptional ability enables a threatened squid to camouflage itself instantly, to the point of near invisibility.

REFLECTION

Nowadays, people routinely villainize those with whom they disagree, and even go after them with violence. If you become one of their targets, you can suddenly find yourself in grave danger.

Historically, the adherents of most major religions have faced periods of precisely that kind of hateful brutality. During Nero's rule over the Roman Empire, Christians were fed to the lions for sport. During Hitler's reign of terror, Jews were incinerated by the millions.

There are many ways to protect yourself from such danger. For instance, you might quickly flee from it, like a squid jet-propelling itself away from a deadly sperm whale.

You might hide yourself in plain sight by first assimilating into a hostile society and then becoming an influencer, the way the apostle Paul did. Or hide in a safe space, the way Anne Frank and seven others did for twenty-five months in the secret annex in Amsterdam.

You might camouflage yourself, as many early Christians did throughout the Mediterranean, and as many Christians do today who live in countries hostile to their beliefs.

Or you might stay and fight. Stand up against those who would cancel or even kill you for what you believe.

Which choice would you make?

THE CREATOR SPEAKS

When I was with the Jews, I lived like a Jew. . . . When I am with the Gentiles who do not follow the Jewish law, I too live apart from that law. . . . When I am with those who are weak, I share their weakness. . . . Yes, I try to find common ground with everyone, doing everything I can to save some . . . to spread the Good News and share in its blessings.

1 CORINTHIANS 9:20-23

119

Buried Treasure

On April 15, 1912, the supposedly unsinkable RMS *Titanic*—on its maiden voyage across the North Atlantic from Southampton to New York City—collided with an iceberg and sank 12,000 feet to the bottom of the ocean. More than 1,500 people died, leaving only about 700 survivors—making it the deadliest cruise ship disaster ever during peacetime.

Among the *Titanic*'s ultra-wealthy, first-class passengers were some of the who's who of high society. When they went down, their prized possessions went down with them.

Over the years, salvage crews and treasure hunters have successfully recovered some of the valuables, including an 18 carat diamond-and-platinum ring, a gold pocket watch, and a large trove of expensive brooches, necklaces, and cuff links.

One expedition tried to salvage an entire, twenty-ton section of the *Titanic*. They almost succeeded, but at the last minute—just several hundred feet from the surface—the ropes snapped and the section sank back to the seafloor.

Many people regard all such recovery efforts as desecrations of a burial site and have called for them to stop. In 2019, the United Kingdom and United States signed a treaty aimed at protecting the *Titanic*'s wreckage from further looting, but it's questionable whether it can be enforced.

Meanwhile, the wreck of the *Titanic* is facing yet another ignominy—this one so small it can be seen only through a microscope. It's a unique salt-water-loving bacteria, named after the *Titanic*, that actually feeds on iron: *Halomonas titanicae*.

Scientists discovered the microscopic critters on icicles made of rust, called *rusticles*, salvaged from the *Titanic*. At the rate *H. titanicae* is chomping away at the wreck, scientists estimate the vaunted, unsinkable

Titanic—in its day, the largest, most opulent passenger liner ever built—will be completely gone in just twenty or thirty years.

REFLECTION

Most of the world's industrialized nations are dominated by materialistic, secular cultures. Their people are constantly solicited to buy this or that, with glib promises that the consumables will make them happy.

Truth is, the latest shiny objects and the newest trendy gizmos won't ever make us happy, but they will make someone else rich at our expense. Deep down, we know that; yet we keep buying up *stuff* as if there's no tomorrow.

One day, for all of us, there will be no tomorrow. Like those who went down with the *Titanic*, we'll wave goodbye to this world and leave behind all our prized possessions for others to inherit, plunder, or simply throw away.

And then what? What will become of us?

The Bible urges us to invest in the future—in our existence beyond the grave—not by building up storehouses of stuff, but by investing in our relationship with the one who made us and loves us. The one we'll see face-to-face and who won't be impressed with how many toys we accumulated during our short years on Earth.

THE CREATOR SPEAKS

Don't store up treasures here on earth, where moths eat them and rust destroys them, and where thieves break in and steal. Store your treasures in heaven, where moths and rust cannot destroy, and thieves do not break in and steal.

MATTHEW 6:19-20

Hard-Shelled Love

Believe it or not, scientists can tell a lot about an animal's parenting style by the kind of eggs it lays. In particular, by the *hardness* of the eggshells.

Animals that lay hard-shelled eggs are best described as *hands-on* parents. These parents, which include most bird species, sit on their eggs until they hatch; feed the hatchings until they fledge; then teach the fledglings how to feed themselves until they're ready to fly off and go it alone.

Animals that lay soft-shelled eggs are best described as *hands-off* parents. These parents—which include most reptiles, such as alligators, turtles, and snakes—usually find convenient, safe locations to bury their leathery eggs; then walk, crawl, or slither away, leaving their offspring to fend for themselves.

Dinosaurs have presented a real headache to science. For a long while, paleontologists believed the extinct giants were cold-blooded reptiles that, unlike other reptiles, laid hard-shelled eggs.

They had it all wrong.

Based on closer examinations of dinosaur fossils—primarily bones and eggs—scientists now believe that dinosaurs were actually warm-blooded animals that laid *soft*-shelled eggs.

This monumental revelation came in 1995, when Yale scientists analyzed a cluster of dinosaur embryos from the Gobi Desert. They did not find any vestige of calcium, a chemical signature of hard-shelled eggs. Instead, they found halos around the embryos, which spectral analysis revealed contained the chemical signatures of soft-shelled eggs.

Such research has radically altered our view of dinosaurs. Instead of seeing them as doting parents, we now believe the extinct giants simply laid their eggs and ambled away without looking back.

REFLECTION

There are many belief systems in the world, each with its own concept of a supreme being or beings. Most of the deities are like *hands-off* parents; but one of them—the God described in the Bible—is very much like a *hands-on* parent.

Whether you're a Christian or not, that's both good news and not-so-good news.

Hands-off parents offer their offspring a lot of freedom. The kids can do whatever they want without the worry of any parental correction.

As a hands-on parent, the God of the Bible also, too, offers his offspring a lot of freedom—complete freedom, actually. he will also intervene if he sees us going off the rails.

To the more self-absorbed among us, this process of correction is seen as punishment, pure and simple. But to others, it's much more complicated than that.

They recognize that God's corrections, though never pleasant—for him or for us—are true blessings. Reminders, albeit often painful ones, that God loves us enough to keep us from becoming our own worst enemies.

THE CREATOR SPEAKS

My child, don't make light of the LORD's discipline.... For the LORD disciplines those he loves ... so that we might share in his holiness. No discipline is enjoyable while it is happening—it's painful! But afterward there will be a peaceful harvest of right living for those who are trained in this way.

HEBREWS 12:5-6, 10-11

Like a Weed

At the 1876 Centennial Exposition in Philadelphia, botanists presented kudzu (*Pueraria montana*), an Asian perennial vine, as an ideal way to shade porches. Decades later, in the 1930s, the US government proclaimed kudzu as an ideal plant to control erosion and nutrify soil, and they distributed more than 160 million kudzu seedlings for free to Southern farmers and homeowners.

Several decades later, with millions of Southern acres now overrun with kudzu, everyone began to realize their enormous blunder. The once-celebrated legume was now being roundly condemned as "the vine that ate the South."

In the warm, moist climate of the Southeastern US—far away from the checks and balances imposed on it by the climate, flora, and fauna of its native land—kudzu grows up to a foot a day. Once planted, its roots send out runners, each of which branches out in all directions, rapidly creating a vast, almost impenetrable vegetative tangle.

In no time, kudzu smothers the plants and trees all around it, thereby eliminating its competitors for sun and soil. It then goes on to enrobe just about everything else in its path: houses, cars, powerlines, you name it.

Worse still, kudzu is resistant to most herbicides. Killing it often requires many applications of poisonous chemicals, which indiscriminately kill other plants in the same area.

In 1997, Congress officially declared kudzu a noxious weed injurious to agriculture, ecosystems, and livestock. But it was too little, too late; the damage was already done.

Today, the American South remains smothered in kudzu. What's more, despite science's best efforts and the government's belated edicts, it's not likely that Southerners will ever rid themselves of the once-hailed miracle vine.

REFLECTION

Have you ever overeaten something you love? Or been away from home and, free from your normal checks and balances, behaved in some excessive way? If so, you probably sat back afterward, filled with regret, and uttered that familiar truism: "Too much of a good thing is not good."

In the Bible, even King Solomon—one of the wisest, most powerful people of his day—bitterly lamented his addiction to overindulgence. "Anything I wanted, I would take. I denied myself no pleasure. I even found great pleasure in hard work. . . . But as I looked at everything I had worked so hard to accomplish, it was all so meaningless—like chasing the wind."[1]

Many ancient Greek philosophers—Plato, for one—elaborated on the dangers of excess and the virtues of moderation. They lived by the Greek motto *"pan metron ariston"*—everything in moderation.

Whether it's a holiday, hobby, career, friendship, or even a romantic relationship, anything in excess usually leads to trouble. Before you know it, seemingly healthy pleasures morph into noxious weeds that, like kudzu, suffocate the life out of everything near and dear to you.

They become, as the saying goes, too much of a good thing.

THE CREATOR SPEAKS

You say, "I am allowed to do anything"—but not everything is good for you. And even though "I am allowed to do anything," I must not become a slave to anything.

1 CORINTHIANS 6:12

Surviving in Utter Darkness

In 2021, British geologists melted a half-mile-deep hole all the way through the Antarctic's Filchner-Ronne Ice Shelf, excited to study the seafloor sediments hidden beneath it. However, when they lowered their sampling device to the bottom—together with a small video camera—it came back empty-handed.

Puzzled, they examined the video of the trip down and were shocked to discover two things. First, against all odds, instead of hitting soft sediment, their drilling had struck solid rock. And second, the rock was covered with life—primarily bacteria and tiny, cylindrical sponges.

How was this possible? How could life exist in a place buried under thousands of feet of ice, devoid of any sunlight and any perceivable food source?

Back in 1977, marine scientists had discovered life thriving around hot-water geysers at the bottom of the Pacific Ocean (see Invitation 23). Even though there's no sunlight down there, the geysers provide the creatures with plenty of nutritious, life-sustaining minerals.

Scientists had also discovered sea creatures in total darkness that live solely by eating what's called marine snow, dead organisms and detritus that constantly rain down to the seafloor from the ocean's upper, sun-splashed layers.

But creatures that live without sunlight, geysers, or food? Impossible!

To this day, scientists simply don't understand how the Antarctic rock creatures can possibly survive in utter, ice-cold darkness.

They also don't know something else: Are these rock creatures rare or the norm beneath Antarctica's 5.4 million square miles of thick ice? To date, we've only been able to dig down and explore a few thousand square feet—approximately the size of a tennis court—of the giant continent's ice covering.

Until we're able to explore a larger area than that, the mystery of Antarctica's rock creatures will remain deeply concealed from us.

REFLECTION

There may be times in your life when you feel very much like one of those rock creatures. You feel weighed down by a massive burden; suffering alone in an emotionally cold, dark place, desperate for the nourishment of love and the light of hope.

How do you survive such soul-crushing conditions, especially if it goes on and on and on, without any sign of letting up? Not easily, or at all, if you don't find nourishment and light from something or someone other than yourself.

Perhaps there's a family member or friend who can meet those vital needs. But even then, no human alone can hold out for very long before they, too, succumb to the terrifying, bone-chilling darkness of your crisis.

According to the Bible, there's only one limitless source of nourishment and light, of love and hope, in the universe: God. If you call out to him from your utter, despairing darkness—reach out to him with a sincere, confident expectation that he'll answer—he will (gradually or instantly) melt away the mountain of ice that's crushing you and will revive you with a spiritual nourishment that science cannot possibly explain.

THE CREATOR SPEAKS

Rejoice in our confident hope. Be patient in trouble, and keep on praying.

ROMANS 12:12

Out of Sight

For centuries, astronomers assumed that everything we could see in the heavens—planets, moons, stars—were all that existed; there was nothing more. But that assumption proved to be wrong. *Very* wrong.

Today, astronomers realize that the universe we see—even with our most powerful telescopes—is but a tiny, tiny fraction of what is actually out there. They now realize there's a vast, unseen realm ruled by mighty, unseen, dark forces that science knows next to nothing about.

This eye-popping discovery was made in the 1930s, when a Swiss-American scientist named Fritz Zwicky noticed something strange: Galaxy clusters were spinning much faster than expected. This discrepancy implies that the clusters—and individual galaxies themselves—are far more massive than they appear. Scientists now surmise that galaxies contain surplus material totally invisible and inexplicable to us. We call it *dark matter*.

In 1998, scientists discovered something even stranger: The universe is not only expanding—like a giant, inflatable, four-dimensional beach ball—it's expanding at an ever-increasing rate as well. In other words, the cosmic expansion is *accelerating*.

Think about your car. To make it accelerate, you need to step on the gas, right? So, what's stepping on the gas to make the universe accelerate? Scientists don't know—it's a deep mystery—but they've come up with a name for it: *dark energy*.

Based on our newest measurements, we now believe the universe is roughly 68 percent dark energy and 27 percent dark matter. This means only 5 percent of the cosmos is actually visible to us and our mightiest instruments.

REFLECTION

Whenever your life is upended by trials and tribulations, you naturally look around, back, or inward for someone or something to blame. But God sees far more than you do. He sees it *all*—not just the conspicuous culprits, but the covert ones as well.

You cannot fight what you cannot see. That's why God is there for you. If you let him, he will help you defeat the invisible dark forces of the universe warring against you this very minute.

THE CREATOR SPEAKS

We are not fighting against flesh-and-blood enemies, but against evil rulers and authorities of the unseen world, against mighty powers in this dark world, and against evil spirits in the heavenly places.
EPHESIANS 6:12

Bubble of Protection

The diving bell spider (*Argyroneta aquatica*) is the only known spider that spends its entire life underwater. These unique spiders live throughout Europe and Asia in ponds, shallow lakes, marshes, slow-flowing rivers, and other bodies of calm, fresh water.

A diving bell spider—which, like all arachnids, needs air to survive—starts its life by diving underwater and weaving a tightly knitted, dome-shaped, silk web that's anchored to an aquatic plant. The web looks like a classic diving bell.

Next, the spider heads to the surface, where it pokes its back end out of the water. Fine hairs on its hind legs and belly capture a tiny bubble of air.

The spider then dives back down and releases the bubble into the silk diving bell, where it is held captive. The spider repeats this routine many times in order to build up—bubble by bubble—an air chamber large enough to accommodate its whole body.

The spider spends the entire winter hibernating inside the life-supporting air chamber. During the rest of the year, it sits inside it, waiting and watching for prey.

If for any reason it needs to leave the air chamber for a significant length of time, the spider takes with it a tiny air bubble. As it swims around, it looks every bit like a scuba diver packing an Aqua-Lung.

REFLECTION

Like diving bell spiders, we live in a world—in our case, a man-made world—hostile to our existence. A world constantly threatening to drown us in wickedness.

In order to survive, we need the equivalent of the diving bell spider's dome-shaped web. An "air chamber" filled with God's powerful, life-giving Spirit.

Unlike diving bell spiders, however, we don't have to create it. The Bible explains that God offers it to us for free.

The temptations you face daily—minute by minute—are often too great to overcome on your own. They constantly threaten to swamp you, just as water does to a diving bell spider. It's only by safely ensconcing yourself in the Spirit—by maintaining a close relationship with God—that you stand any chance of not drowning.

THE CREATOR SPEAKS

> God is our refuge and strength,
>   always ready to help in times of trouble....
> Let the oceans roar and foam.
>   Let the mountains tremble as the waters surge!...
>   The God of Israel is our fortress.
>
> PSALM 46:1, 3, 7

Adopted Family

To the untrained eye, common loons (*Gavia immer*) and mallard ducks (*Anas platyrhynchos*) look very similar. Both are duck-like, live in or near water, and have webbed feet.

In truth, though, the two species are very different. Loons are related to pelicans and penguins, whereas mallards are related to chickens and grouses. The result: Loons and mallards are fierce rivals, routinely competing for the best nesting sites.

In 2019, Evelyn Doolittle, a young woman studying loons on more than a hundred lakes in central Wisconsin, made a startling discovery. She spied a mallard chick riding atop a full-grown female loon.

Upon further investigation, Doolittle determined that the baby mallard had been fully adopted into a loon family. It was something scientists had never seen before.

The loon parents cared for the mallard chick as if it were one of their own biological offspring. They fed it minnows and other fish, and the baby gobbled it all down, even though mallards generally eat only vegetation and insects.

The loon parents also taught the baby duck to dive, a behavior wholly uncommon to mallards. All in all, Doolittle's discovery shocked the research community, because even though interspecies adoptions do occur, they're extremely rare—especially between rival species.

REFLECTION

As described in the book of Genesis, we and God have been rivals from the very beginning. It isn't how God had hoped it would be, but our constant rebelliousness has put enormous distance between us and our loving creator.

Still, God hasn't given up on us—not by a long shot. Even today, after all that's happened, he offers to adopt us into his divine family.

When you accept the offer, he teaches you behaviors unlike those of a typical, worldly person. Whether it's how much you eat, how you dress, how you see yourself and others, these new behaviors reflect the biblical concept that you are a holy creature.

Above all, the rivalry you once felt with God disappears. In its place is the inexpressible comfort that comes from being held in God's arms, and the incomparable view that comes from seeing the world through our adopted parent's eyes.

THE CREATOR SPEAKS

You have not received a spirit that makes you fearful slaves. Instead, you received God's Spirit when he adopted you as his own children. Now we call him, "Abba, Father."
ROMANS 8:15

A Constant Irritation

Every dazzling gemstone—be it a diamond, ruby, sapphire, you name it—is formed over a very long time and under great pressure within the earth's crust. With one exception: *pearls*.

A pearl forms inside a mussel or an oyster through a very unlikely process.

It begins when an irritant of some kind—a grain of sand, small stone, or parasite—manages to work its way into the creature's clammed-up interior. The mussel or oyster instantly reacts by smothering the irritant with layer upon layer of a thick substance called *nacre*.

Nacre is a viscous fluid made of shimmering, calcium carbonate crystals and a glue-like protein called conchiolin. Because it gives birth to all pearls, nacre is also called *mother-of-pearl*.

A typical pearl takes about six months to three years to fully develop and harden. Larger, rarer ones naturally take longer.

One of the largest pearls in the world was discovered in 2006 by Filipino fishermen whose boat anchor got stuck on the sea bottom just before a storm. After yanking on the rope without success, one of the fishermen dove into the choppy waters and discovered that the anchor had gotten stuck on a giant clam.

After freeing the anchor, the men hauled the huge creature up and onto their boat. With enormous effort, they pried open the mammoth clamshell and were shocked at what was inside: a colossal, knobby shaped, iridescent pearl weighing a record seventy-five pounds!

The monster-sized pearl is currently on display inside New Green City Hall in Puerto Princesa, the Philippines. Its value is still being estimated; but in 2003, a fourteen-pound beauty called the Pearl of Lao Tzu was valued at $93 million. By that reckoning, the Puerto Princesa pearl—the stunning product of a constant irritation—is estimated to be worth $130 million.[1]

REFLECTION

Rhonda Spencer-Hwang, a professor of public health at California's Loma Linda University, wrote a book called *Raising Resilient Kids*.[2] In it she summarizes her research on centenarians, people who have enjoyed unusually long, successful lives. Her biggest discovery: Far from having privileged upbringings, these exceptional people had extremely rigorous, difficult childhoods.

Those very rigors and difficulties, Dr. Spencer-Hwang determined, helped make the centenarians resilient. And that resilience, in turn, helped them not only survive, but *thrive* for more than a century.

The Bible reports that the apostle Paul constantly suffered from a "thorn" in his flesh—a nagging irritation that, despite Paul's pleading, God did not remove. But rather than being angry at God for the irritation, or throwing up his hands and quitting, Paul pursued a tireless, world-changing ministry. What's more, he actually credited the thorn in his side for keeping him from getting too full of himself.[3]

Is there something or someone who this very minute is a thorn in your side? Does it—or do they—constantly bring out the worst in you? If so, it doesn't have to be that way.

As the spectacular pearl of Puerto Princesa, Dr. Spencer-Hwang's extraordinary centenarians, and the inimitable apostle Paul exemplify: A constant irritation in life can actually bring out the *best and most beautiful* in you.

THE CREATOR SPEAKS

Count it all joy . . . when you meet trials of various kinds, for you know that the testing of your faith produces steadfastness. And let steadfastness have its full effect, that you may be perfect and complete, lacking in nothing.

JAMES 1:2-4, ESV

Power Up!

To most people, a storm cloud is merely a dark, ominous blob of water vapor. In reality, though, it is a monstrous power plant capable of generating lightning strokes brighter than three million 60-watt light bulbs. Jagged spears of light that heat the air to 50,000°F—five times hotter than the sun's surface!

Where does all that power come from?

Ironically, it comes from the cloud's tiny water droplets rubbing against each other, liberating countless electrons. That frictional process creates sparks, just like someone who walks across a woolen carpet in hard rubber-soled shoes or runs a comb through dry hair.

The sparks inside a storm cloud start small. But as the static electricity builds and builds, it ultimately produces lightning bolts—sparks so enormous they reach all the way to the ground.

For years, scientists used aircraft and weather balloons to estimate the total power of a storm cloud. Based on those measurements, they estimated that a typical storm cloud is comparable to a 200-million-watt power plant.

In 2014, however, scientists used an entirely different technique, and the result was shocking. According to the new estimate, a typical storm cloud is actually comparable to a *two-billion-watt* power plant.

That means the average storm cloud floating above your head carries the same punch as a large nuclear or hydroelectric power station. All because of tiny water droplets rubbing against each other!

REFLECTION

The energy you need to stay alive comes from many different sources: food, air, water, you name it. Without them, your body would quickly give out.

Your spirit, however, is a different matter. According to the Bible, your spirit is powered not by calories, but by your creator, God himself.

God's voice alone generates more wattage than is contained in all the storm clouds on Earth—in all the universe. After all, he spoke everything into being.

His power is so unimaginably mighty that it also breaks the strict rules governing the ordinary, physical universe. Like a perpetual motion machine—forbidden by the laws of physics—God's spiritual power is eternal; it never runs down.

Successfully connect with such an indescribable power source and you'll be struck by a bolt of spiritual lightning. It will energize you in this life and also open your eyes to the next one.

THE CREATOR SPEAKS

I pray that from his glorious, unlimited resources he will empower you with inner strength through his Spirit.
EPHESIANS 3:16

137

Life from Death

For most people, the word *fungus* has understandably negative connotations. After all, fungi—bizarre organisms that are neither plant nor animal—cause many horrific and deadly afflictions.

In many ways, however, we owe our very lives to fungi. For starters, they are in lots of our most delicious, healthy foods, such as yeasts, mushrooms, and truffles.

Also, fungi actually protect us from many lethal illnesses. The famous antibiotic penicillin, discovered in 1928 by Alexander Fleming, a Scottish physician, is made from a fungus—specifically, a mold from the genus *Penicillium*.

Above all, fungi are phenomenal recyclers. They love eating dead things—dead leaves, dead wood, dead animals—breaking them down to their essential chemicals.

These liberated chemicals spread far and wide to re-nutrify the earth, keeping its flora well fed, which in turn keeps its fauna—including you—well fed. In this way, fungi play a huge role in keeping our entire planet fat and happy.

Rob Dunn, a biologist in the department of applied ecology at North Carolina State University, summarizes the surprising importance of fungi beautifully: "[The earth's] entire web of life is connected . . . through the fungi. It's how everything is reborn."[1]

REFLECTION

We all have parts of our lives that are dead or dying. Maybe it's a stalled career, or the premature loss of a loved one, or a dreadful addiction.

If left alone, all those dead and dying burdens in your life will bury you. Beneath their enormous weight, you'll be unable to move anymore. Or feel anymore. Or care anymore.

The only way out from under the load is with outside help. With *God's* help.

The Bible explains: Ask God for help and he will transform your mountain of deathly burdens into a stack of life-changing opportunities, akin to a fungus that transforms a pile of smelly carcasses into a heap of life-giving nutrients.

THE CREATOR SPEAKS

Let the Spirit renew your thoughts and attitudes. Put on your new nature, created to be like God—truly righteous and holy.
EPHESIANS 4:23-24

A Mysterious Light

For centuries, scientists believed that physical objects fall into two basic categories: *rocks* and *ripples*. Rock-like objects have a definite shape and move in one direction at a time—such as planets, BBs, and bacteria. Ripple-like objects are smeared out and often fan out in various directions at once—like an ocean wave, a gust of wind, or a blast of sound.

The perennial problem child with this theory is *light*. Is it rock-like? Or ripple-like?

In the early nineteenth century, British polymath Thomas Young did an experiment that clearly showed light to be ripple-like. Decades later, the German physicist Heinrich Hertz did an experiment that clearly showed light to be rock-like.

What?!

It wasn't until the early twentieth century that the legendary German physicist Albert Einstein concluded that light appears to defy the age-old, two-bucket dogma. Light, he proposed, is *quantum*-like, a mysterious, hitherto unknown category of reality that's both fully rock-like *and* fully ripple-like.

Einstein's light quantum seemed as illogical as something claiming to be fully black *and* fully white, fully even *and* fully odd, fully real *and* fully unreal. Nevertheless, Einstein's quantum couldn't be dismissed as nonsense; instead, we soon discovered it was a *translogical* truth, a real-life phenomenon that completely defies logic.

In 1954, an aged Einstein wrote to his good friend Michele Besso, confessing: "All these fifty years of conscious brooding have brought me no nearer to the answer to the question, 'What are light quanta?' Nowadays every Tom, Dick and Harry thinks he knows it, but he is mistaken."[1]

To this day, no one is able to comprehend a light quantum. By their very nature, translogical objects and concepts are impossible to imagine.

Nevertheless, comprehensible or not, Einstein's puzzling quantum remains the rock-ripple foundation of modern physics.

REFLECTION

The New Testament is filled with references to realities that completely defy logic and common sense. For example, Jesus asserts that the greatest is the least; the first will be last; and that in order to keep your life you must lose it. He urges us to love our enemies; bless our persecutors; and give generously to those who wish to take everything from us!

These upside-down truths sound illogical, but they can't be dismissed as nonsense. Like Einstein's light quantum, Jesus' teachings are *translogical*.

Jesus himself is translogical. According to the Bible, he is the progeny both of an immortal God *and* of a very mortal, teenage virgin.

How can that be? How can Jesus be both immortal and mortal? Fully God and fully man? Answer: the same way a light quantum can be fully rock-like and fully ripple-like.

Indeed, according to the Bible, the fundamental nature of God—of Jesus—is identical to the fundamental nature of light. God, like light, is unimaginable and incomprehensible; yet like light, he's also very real.

THE CREATOR SPEAKS

This is the message we heard from Jesus and now declare to you: God is light, and there is no darkness in him at all.
1 JOHN 1:5

Coat of Many Colors

Polar bears (*Ursus maritimus*), mighty carnivores of land and sea, live primarily in the cold, snowy environs of the Arctic. But there's one thing about them that might surprise you: Despite being famous for their bright, white appearance (which makes for perfect camouflage), they're not actually white at all.

In fact, their skin is black, and they're covered from head to toe by an inner layer of short, plush hairs and an outer layer of long hairs—all of which are *colorless*.

What's more, the long, outer hairs are hollow. When struck by sunlight, which comprises all the colors of the rainbow, the rough interiors of the hollow hairs scatter the colors equally, creating the net impression of bright, white light.

Because it's an optical illusion, the whiteness of a polar bear's coat is subject to change. On a cloudy day, its hair can appear grayish; during a spectacular sunset, reddish-orange; or at the end of spring, yellowish, due to the staining of oily seal fat, the bear's main food source.

Polar bears can even look green. Yes, *green*.

During the summer of 1978, this startling natural phenomenon created quite a sensation at the world-famous San Diego Zoo. The hair on three of its bears suddenly turned a sickly shade of green.[1]

Vets examined the bears and found them to be in perfect health. In the process, however, they discovered the root of the mystery: The bears' hollow hairs had filled with water that, in the summer heat, had grown slimy, green algae. It was unsightly, and it scared visitors at the zoo, but the algae was not harmful to the bears' health.

When Arctic temperatures peak during the summer months, even polar bears in the wild can turn green—especially across their flanks, legs, and rumps. It makes the bears stand out, and it's therefore harder for them to sneak up on prey; but luckily for the mighty hunters, they shed their hair every summer, so every fall they return to looking white as snow.

REFLECTION

Like most people, you probably behave differently in different settings. Kids are especially notorious for behaving like angels under the watchful eye of their parents and like little devils when hanging out with their besties. Some people may be kind to your face but insulting behind your back.

Adapting to our circumstances isn't a bad thing. There's nothing wrong with being quiet and respectful at a funeral or rowdy at a pool party. Or choosing not to be "completely honest" when to do so might damage a relationship.

But if we try to appear to be something we're not, in order to get something we want, our duplicity betrays insincerity—or, worse, sinister intentions. Like an all-white polar bear sneaking up on a hapless seal, camouflaging our true intentions can make us dangerous to the people in our lives.

How often do you change your public persona to disguise your motives? Are you a "different person" from one setting to the next, or do you maintain a consistent persona? Are you all smiles when you want something from someone, but stone-faced when someone wants something from you? Or is your behavior consistently open, forthright, and generous?

"Just being yourself" can all too often be used as an excuse for outspoken and obnoxious behavior. Instead, strive to be your *best* self, always and everywhere.

THE CREATOR SPEAKS

Do not drag me away with the wicked—
*   with those who do evil—*
those who speak friendly words to their neighbors
*   while planning evil in their hearts.*
PSALM 28:3

143

Heart Transplant

Giraffes (*Giraffa camelopardalis*), the tallest land animals in the world, can grow to be nineteen feet tall. Their spectacular necks and legs alone are each six feet long.

Pumping blood to such heights requires a huge, powerful heart. On average a giraffe's heart is two feet long and weighs a whopping twenty-four-plus pounds. By comparison, a human heart weighs less than one pound.

The giraffe's giant heart pumps at a rate of 170 beats per minute and creates a blood pressure of 280/180. That's roughly twice the rate and pressure of a human heart.

As big as a giraffe's heart is, however, cardiologists originally expected it to be much bigger, given the animal's gigantic stature and weight. But they soon discovered the reason for the heart's unexpectedly small size: Its left ventricle (the lower left chamber that does the heavy lifting, pumping blood throughout the animal's massive body) has a muscular wall that's unusually thick and powerful.

In a healthy human, the left-ventricular wall is no more than about 0.4 inches thick. In a healthy giraffe, the same wall is *seven times* as thick.

A paper published in the prestigious scientific journal *Nature* summarized this surprising revelation exceedingly well. In every respect, its authors proclaimed, a giraffe's heart is "turbocharged."[1]

REFLECTION

In 1982, surgeons at the University of Utah made worldwide headlines by becoming the first to transplant a permanent artificial heart into a human being. The clunky, air-powered heart—the so-called *Jarvik-7*, named for its principal coinventor, Dr. Robert Jarvik—kept sixty-one-year-old Seattle dentist Barney Clark alive for 112 days.

Today, scientists are scrambling to develop artificial hearts that can keep patients alive for longer periods of time. But even the best among them—currently, a thirteen-pound pneumatic-driven contraption that a patient carries around on a shoulder strap—are a far cry from a natural human heart. And an even farther cry from a giraffe's remarkable heart.

Beyond hearts made of plastic and metal, and even of flesh and blood, is the heart described in the Bible. It's a spiritual organ that pumps love, light, and life into every relationship you have.

So, then, today I challenge you with this question: What's the condition of your spiritual heart?

Is it small and weak, so that it's able to pump just enough love, light, and life to sustain your own selfish desires? Or is it colossal and giraffe-like, so that it can nurture healthy relationships with diverse people, far and wide—and even with God, as high up as heaven?

THE CREATOR SPEAKS

I will give you a new heart, and I will put a new spirit in you.
I will take out your stony, stubborn heart and give you a tender,
responsive heart.
EZEKIEL 36:26

Providential Provisions

Many birds find food in the strangest places and in the strangest ways. They do so either because they have no choice or because that's how they're designed.

Take, for example, Australia's Bassian thrush (*Zoothera lunulata*). This secretive, olive-brown bird hops across fields, pausing and probing the soil with its beak for earthworms and other bugs, just like an American robin.

But there's a twist.

In 1983, an Australian ornithologist named J. S. L. Edington published a startling—and to this day controversial—observation: While hopping, pausing, and probing for worms, the Bassian thrush passes gas strategically.

Here's how Edington put it: "A noise similar to a jet of air . . . (clearly audible at five metres and lasting less than 0.25 sec.) . . . was produced immediately after stopping and was in turn, followed by probing or more hopping."[1]

Why in the world does the Bassian thrush resort to this foraging flatulence? In Edington's own words: "[It] may well be a 'scare tactic' to induce earthworms to contract reflexly . . . and so betray their presence to the Thrush through noise or litter movement and vibration."[2]

Another odd bird is northern Eurasia's western capercaillie (*Tetrao urogallus*). Approximately the size of an American turkey—with dark brown, gray, and metallic-green feathers—it's the largest of all existing grouses.

Given its large size, you'd expect the capercaillie to be constantly stuffing its face with hearty meals; but that's not so. Throughout the long, desolate winter months, it survives solely by eating pine needles!

Then there's the Cuban tody (*Todus multicolor*), a small rainbow-colored bird with a black and red beak. Being small, a tody readily loses body heat, which means it must eat and eat and eat to stay warm and alive.

On average, todies eat about 40 percent of their body weight *every day*—mostly bugs, but also seeds and berries. When feeding their chicks—which they do about 140 times per day!—adult todies must forage for that much more food. During a typical, six-month feeding season, a single tody family will consume roughly 1.8 million insects.

REFLECTION

The Bible explains that God is not a genie: He doesn't always give you what you want, in the way you want it, at the time you want it. But he always gives you what you need when you need it—just as he does for his beloved birds.

But there's a huge difference between us and birds. We often reject God's providential provisions because they aren't what we asked for—birds are smarter, less rebellious than that.

Don't be unwise, be more like the birds of the air. Even when you're struggling through a severe winter season in life, and all you have amounts to a heap of pine needles, accept them gratefully; because God promises that his well-timed provisions will always get you through to the following spring.

THE CREATOR SPEAKS

Look at the birds in the sky! They don't plant or harvest. They don't even store grain in barns. Yet your Father in heaven takes care of them. Aren't you worth much more than birds?
MATTHEW 6:26, CEV

Seeing the Unseeable

Neptune, the eighth planet from the sun, is blue and frigid. It constantly experiences winds of up to 1,200 miles per hour, the fiercest on any planet in our solar system.

Neptune is so far away we can't see it without a telescope. But thanks to photos taken by the long-distance *Voyager 2* spacecraft, we know that Neptune orbits the sun once every 165 earth years and has six rings and fourteen moons.

We discovered the existence of Neptune in a most unusual, indirect way. In 1781, astronomers noticed a slight wobble in the orbit of Uranus—at the time, the farthest planet we knew about—and wondered: *What's causing that?*

In 1846, French astronomer and mathematician Urbain Jean-Joseph Le Verrier speculated that the wobble was caused by the pull of an unknown planet *beyond* Uranus. Le Verrier sent the approximate coordinates of this hypothesized planet to astronomers at the Berlin Observatory. They, in turn, pointed their telescope to those coordinates and—*lo!*—there it was, Le Verrier's planet. It was eventually named Neptune, after the ancient Roman god of the sea.

REFLECTION

Just as Le Verrier inferred the existence of Neptune from its effects on Uranus, we can infer God's existence from the effects he has on people. And also from everything science is discovering about the universe.

From the microscopic to the astronomical, the more science reveals about the cosmos, the less it appears to be a grand and glorious accident. Indeed, based on everything we're able to see—and not see, but detect—the universe appears to be intentionally made for life. For *us*.

The Bible, too, is a powerful telescope of sorts. Through its powerful lens—its pages of sacred Scripture—we behold the image of a powerful deity who embodies love, light, and life.

He's the brains behind the nebulas, stars, and planets that light up the night sky like diamonds. Behind our solar system. Behind the sun, moons, and planets, including Neptune.

He's the incomprehensible mind behind all life on planet Earth, and wherever else life might exist. Behind the plants and animals that enrich our lives in so many different ways.

Above all, we can infer from everything science and the Bible teaches us that he's the awesome-yet-approachable creator responsible for making *you*.

THE CREATOR SPEAKS

Ever since the world was created, people have seen the earth and sky. Through everything God made, they can clearly see his invisible qualities—his eternal power and divine nature. So they have no excuse for not knowing God.

ROMANS 1:20

Icebreaker

Earth's polar regions are cold year-round, but especially during their respective winters. In the Arctic, the average winter temperature is -4°C (24.8°F); in the Antarctic, the coldest continent on the planet, it's -59.5°C (-75.1°F).

It's shocking, therefore, to see vast regions of ice-free, relatively warm-water oases in the midst of this frigidity. These year-round resorts, called *polynyas*, are a godsend to polar bears, walruses, seals, belugas, arctic cod, narwhals, penguins, and scores of other wildlife.

The processes that create polynyas are not fully understood. But as far as scientists can tell, polynyas come in two varieties.

The first are *latent-heat* polynyas, which are typically hundreds of miles long. They're created by strong offshore winds that constantly blow away any ice covering the sea along the coastline.

The exposed seawater quickly freezes; but when water freezes, it releases heat—what scientists call the *latent heat of freezing*. That excess heat, combined with the offshore winds, create polynyas that stay ice-free and relatively warm. Not exactly hot tubs, but comfy enough to attract lots of creatures.

The second kind are *sensible-heat* polynyas, which exist well away from shore. Their exact cause still eludes us, but we think it's warm, deep water rising up and melting huge regions of surface ice. These polynyas are typically about sixty miles (one hundred kilometers) across, but they can get much bigger than that.

The sensible-heat Weddell Polynya in the Antarctic, for example. During the winters of 1974 and 1976, it got to be nearly the size of New Zealand!

Large enough to be seen from space.

REFLECTION

There are many reasons why some people's hearts toward God are as cold as the Antarctic in the dead of winter. Maybe he didn't answer a desperate plea the way they wanted; or represents too much of an authority figure; or is, to them, nothing but a childish fantasy.

Christians are naturally eager to proselytize these coldhearted souls—usually with tracts, personal testimonies, extra-biblical evidence, and thoughtful arguments. But another approach is for Christians simply to offer their friendship—without any strings attached, or any agenda, or any plan to convert them.

Remember: Only God—his Holy Spirit—has the power to actually convert anyone. The best thing a Christian can do is to model true Christian behavior.

That means being a living, breathing polynya in a cold, hard world. It means treating everybody—even the most frozen-hearted of them all—with the warmth of God's unconditional love and his amazing grace.

THE CREATOR SPEAKS

You are the light of the world—like a city on a hilltop that cannot be hidden. No one lights a lamp and then puts it under a basket. Instead, a lamp is placed on a stand, where it gives light to everyone in the house. In the same way, let your good deeds shine out for all to see, so that everyone will praise your heavenly Father.

MATTHEW 5:14-16

Wind Power

A season or place or memory is often defined by its windiness.

Nothing says spring, for example, like a soft breeze on a beautiful, warm day. Likewise, nothing says autumn like the colorful leaves of an aspen tree fluttering and shimmering in a bracing gust of air. And nothing is more wondrously mysterious than wind moaning on a snowy, winter night.

In North Texas, where I live, winds are a godsend during the hot summer months. When temperatures soar above 100°F, moderate breezes invariably pick up in the afternoon that make the heat bearable.

Growing up in Los Angeles, however, I always dreaded the notorious Santa Ana winds. They come roaring down from California's mountainous east, usually during the fall. These devil winds, as I call them, are strong, hot, and dry—and they blow nonstop for days at a time.

Above all, though, winds are essential to the health of our planet.

For one thing, they help transport heat from Earth's hot equatorial regions to its cold polar regions. This has the effect of creating vast temperate zones between the equator and the poles, where temperatures are usually never too hot nor too cold, but just right. If the winds were ever to stop blowing, Earth would quickly get too hot or too cold *everywhere*, making it a very unpleasant place to live.

Winds also help keep the planet green. Many seeds in the wild are designed to be spread far and wide by the wind. And pollen grains, light as a feather, ride the winds to impregnate the earth's flowering and fruiting vegetation.

Years ago I was asked, "Which is stronger: water or wind?" I daresay, most people would say that water is stronger, given its superior bulk.

But, in fact, *wind* is stronger. Just think about ocean waves: they're created mostly by wind.

In a head-to-head matchup, in other words, wind pushes water around, not vice versa.

REFLECTION

The Bible likens God's Holy Spirit to a wind, and rightfully so. Like the wind, God's Spirit is invisible, free to come and go as it pleases, and possesses enormous power.

The Bible explains that, back when God first made humans, he breathed air into Adam's lungs. That seminal wind, as it were, had the power to bring Adam to life.

The Bible also speaks about a person being *born again*. It happens when the person invites God to breathe his Holy Spirit into their entire being.

When you are born again, you stop being tossed hither and thither by every random wind or willful impulse. Instead, the Holy Spirit fills your sails with a strong, purposeful wind that steadily drives you toward your God-given destiny.

THE CREATOR SPEAKS

Suddenly, there was a sound from heaven like the roaring of a mighty windstorm, and it filled the house where they were sitting.... And everyone present was filled with the Holy Spirit.
ACTS 2:2, 4

Stinks to
High Heaven

The corpse flower (*Amorphophallus titanum*), a very rare, 300-pound tropical plant native to Indonesia's Sumatran rainforests, consists of two main parts: a giant, tulip-shaped, reddish-purple skirt (spathe) and a yellowish, central stalk (spadix) that can grow to be twenty feet tall.

The plant is spectacularly unusual in other ways as well. It blooms just once every *seven to ten years* and must be pollinated within twenty-four to forty-eight hours of its flowering in order to become fertile.

By far the most staggering feature of this exotic plant, however, is its stinky aroma—which the flower amplifies by heating itself up to 98°F. The smell is so revolting that most people who approach the flower have to hold their nose or wheel around and flee.

By contrast, to carrion beetles (family Silphidae) and flesh flies (family Sarcophagidae)—used to laying their eggs in the rotting flesh of dead animals—the corpse flower smells so heavenly, they're actually *attracted* to it. Once inside the flower, however, the insects quickly realize they've been hoodwinked; but it doesn't matter, because their tiny bodies are already covered in corpse flower pollen, which they then proceed to disperse far and wide.

In a 2010 report published in *Bioscience, Biotechnology and Biochemistry*, scientists identified the specific chemicals responsible for the corpse flower's stench. All together, they comprise a veritable symphony of nature's most repugnant smells, including: dimethyl trisulfide (rotting onions), trimethylamine (rotting fish), and isovaleric acid (old, sweaty socks).

Pee-yoo!

REFLECTION

Inevitably, there have been times in your life when you behaved in ways that left you feeling ashamed. Naturally, you try forgetting such times by stuffing them deep into your subconscious.

But there, out of sight and mind, those shameful experiences can pile up and rot, like so many smelly corpses. Over time, their collective stench can surface in ways that arrest your attention and reconvict you.

You unexpectedly feel an overwhelming sense of remorse, disgust, and depression. You might even begin doubting your goodness and fret that others will smell the real you—or what you now ashamedly *consider* to be the real you.

If you're in such a predicament, the Bible offers you words of encouragement. It explains that God is not put off by your stinky baggage; in fact, he stands ready to embrace you, no matter how bad you smell, or think you smell.

In order for him to do that, though, you must open yourself up to his advances—though, unlike a corpse flower, not just for twenty-four to forty-eight hours once every seven to ten years. You must open up your smelly self to God's loving, life-giving embrace *permanently*, once and for all.

THE CREATOR SPEAKS

We are all infected and impure with sin. When we display our righteous deeds, they are nothing but filthy rags.
ISAIAH 64:6

But if we confess our sins to him, he is faithful and just to forgive us our sins and to cleanse us from all wickedness.
1 JOHN 1:9

Cone-Shaped Reality

In 1905, Albert Einstein shattered science's long-held traditional beliefs about the universe. For many centuries, scientists had believed that physical reality is three-dimensional, and that in principle every bit of it is accessible to us humans.

But according to Einstein's theory of special relativity, physical reality is *four*-dimensional, and most of it is strictly off-limits to us. His theory claims that our entire existence, from birth to death, is confined to the inside of a *light cone*. The surface of the cone and everything outside of it—a realm called *the elsewhere*—is forbidden territory.

According to the theory of special relativity, your light cone moves with you, its flared end always pointing toward your future. The path you take through life, through 4D space-time, is called your *worldline*.

No two worldlines—and no two light cones—are the same, because no two people and their journeys are the same. You, your light cone, and your worldline are unique.

REFLECTION

Einstein's theory of special relativity and the Bible agree that there's far more to the universe, to reality, than we can ever know in this mortal life.

We live our lives as if we're Truman Burbank, the title character in the movie *The Truman Show*. One day he's shocked to discover he's the star of a reality TV show, and he has spent his entire life inside a sound stage, beyond which is a vast world he never knew existed.

Like Einstein's theory of special relativity, the Bible tells us that a vast, unseen world does, in fact, exist beyond our own. A world that in our present, mortal incarnation, we cannot access or even begin to imagine.

But that's only half the story. According to the Bible, when we die we will break out of our cone-shaped prisons and be able to see the whole of reality in all its awesome vastness and detail.

THE CREATOR SPEAKS

Now we see things imperfectly, like puzzling reflections in a mirror, but then [when we die] we will see everything with perfect clarity. All that I know now is partial and incomplete, but then I will know everything completely, just as God now knows me completely.

1 CORINTHIANS 13:12

Symbiosis

Coral reefs are warm, shallow-water metropolises swarming with crabs, sponges, oysters, urchins, sea stars, and scores of other aquatic life. Even the stony coral reef itself (order Scleractinia) is alive!

A coral reef consists of many stony corals—tiny studio apartments built and inhabited by soft, barrel-shaped, millimeter-sized creatures called *polyps*. They create their stony abodes by ingesting calcium from ocean water and excreting it as calcium carbonate—that is, limestone.

Most of the time, a polyp stays safely indoors, poking out its tentacle-lined mouth only when absolutely necessary—for example, at night to feed. Its tentacles nab and stun any tiny organisms, including zooplankton, that happen to be floating by.

Incredibly, living inside a polyp's stomach tissue are microscopic, photosynthetic algae called *zooxanthellae*. Long ago, the two creatures discovered that each has something invaluable to offer the other—a win-win relationship scientists call *symbiosis*.

Polyps keep the zooxanthellae alive by feeding them carbon dioxide, nitrogen, and phosphates. In return, the algae feed their host polyps oxygen, amino acids, and sugars.

The symbiotic relationship makes stony coral reefs possible. Without it there would be no reefs and therefore no places for countless aquatic life-forms to spawn, grow, hunt, and hide.

And, oh yes, there's a wonderful, surprising bonus to the symbiotic relationship. Polyps by themselves are colorless; the spectacular colors of stony coral reefs come from the colorful, little zooxanthellae living inside the polyps' guts.

REFLECTION

The old saying "No person is an island" could equally read, "No person is a coral reef." Stated plainly: *No one is entirely self-sufficient.*

In countless ways, we all rely on other people, plants, animals, or things to stay alive. Without air, water, food, sunshine, and numerous other sources of sustenance, we would not last long in this world.

And that's not all. If all we do is take, take, take, and not give back, our surroundings—our communities, our ecosystems—will steadily deteriorate until they are completely sucked dry. We must give something back in order for us, and our support systems, to keep going.

The symbiosis between coral polyps and zooxanthellae represents an ideal, life-affirming, give-and-take relationship that we should all strive to emulate. It's one in which we *give* as good as we *get.*

Today, ask yourself and answer honestly: How symbiotic are your relationships with your family, friends, and coworkers? With your neighbors, city, and state? With the insects, birds, and wild creatures that share your piece of the planet?

God calls us to live symbiotically—not just with one another, but with his entire, wondrous creation.

THE CREATOR SPEAKS

Two people are better off than one, for they can help each other succeed. If one person falls, the other can reach out and help. But someone who falls alone is in real trouble.
ECCLESIASTES 4:9-10

Follow the Leader

Ducklings following their mother in a nice, straight line calls to mind elementary schoolkids staying in line during field trips. Keeping youngsters in line is a good way to keep them out of trouble.

In the case of ducks, however, there's more to it than that. Far more.

The first ones to discover this intriguing surprise were scientists from Scotland and China. In a 2021 article in the *Journal of Fluid Mechanics*, they explained that ducklings swim in an orderly queue for very sophisticated, hydrodynamic reasons.

As a mother duck swims through the water, she creates a wake. The details of this wake are such that a duckling following her at just the right distance is sucked along for a near-free ride—up to 62.8 percent of a free ride, to be exact.

When the scientists ran detailed computer models of the situation, they found that the first two ducklings in line behind the mother always benefit most from the hydrodynamic suction. The remaining ducklings benefit to a lesser degree, each one drawn forward by the relatively small wake of the duckling right in front of it.[1]

The scientists discovered one more thing. If the ducklings diverge from a straight line—that is, stray outside the various wakes—then the energy a duckling needs to follow the leader skyrockets.

The ducklings, of course, know nothing about the science of hydrodynamics; but instinctively they do know that following Mom in a straight line makes for a more enjoyable, less exhausting field trip.

REFLECTION

If you're like most people, you like being in control. You wish to be the captain of your destiny, steering your life whichever way you please.

Appealing as that fantasy is to our willful human nature, it's dangerous because no one is smart enough or strong enough to navigate safely through life's choppiest waters. At such times, we all need help from wise family members, friends, professional counselors—above all, from God—to help smooth out the ride.

The Bible describes God's assistance as easy to bear and a source of deep, lasting peace. Agree to follow his lead and you'll feel yourself propelled forward not by a mere hydrodynamic wake, but by God's all-powerful, supernatural wake.

THE CREATOR SPEAKS

Take my yoke upon you. Let me teach you, because I am humble and gentle at heart, and you will find rest for your souls. For my yoke is easy to bear, and the burden I give you is light.

MATTHEW 11:29-30

Inner Beauty

Outward appearances are not always what they seem. The blue morpho butterfly (*Morpho peleides*), native to rain forests in Central, South, and parts of North America, is one of the largest, rarest, most spectacular-looking butterflies in the world. Its wingspan ranges from five to eight inches.

In sunlight, the wings of a male blue morpho are a stunning, iridescent blue. But his true color is actually a dull brown. The blue appearance is produced by diamond-shaped, microscopic scales on the upper-wing surface that preferentially reflect short, blue wavelengths. You might say that sunlight brings out the best in a blue morpho.

The same is true of many other blue colors in nature. The sky, for instance, is really just a cocktail of colorless gases—mainly nitrogen and oxygen. But these molecules selectively scatter blue light—a process called Rayleigh scattering—giving the sky its cherished azure tint.

Other examples of this uncommon optical illusion include common blue jays, blue poison dart frogs, and peacocks. It is sunlight that makes them look blue; in reality, they are unremarkably brown and black.

REFLECTION

If you're like the rest of us, you do and say things you end up regretting. Over time, this bad habit might cause you to have a low opinion of yourself. Worst of all, the more genuine goodness there is in your heart, the more severe your self-reproach is likely to be.

If only you could see yourself as God sees you. He takes into account the great yearnings of your heart—not just what you say and do. He sees not only who you *are*, but who you can become—who he *made* you to be.

Starting today, let him show you what he sees in you. Let him bring out the best in you. Let him transform your self-image from blah to beautiful.

Welcome God into your life, and he will shower you with his supernatural love—like bright sunlight reflecting off your rough edges, producing a stunning beauty seen by everyone who looks upon you.

In the glow of God's love, you'll become as beautiful as a blue morpho fluttering in bright daylight!

THE CREATOR SPEAKS

The LORD does not see as man sees; for man looks at the outward appearance, but the LORD looks at the heart.

1 SAMUEL 16:7, NKJV

Stellar Creation

Kenneth G. Libbrecht, an American physicist at Caltech, is without a doubt the world's foremost authority on snowflakes. His 456-page tome titled *Snow Crystals*—showcasing some of the 10,000-plus photos he's taken of snowflakes over the years—is the undisputed bible on the subject.[1]

Snowflakes, though common, are actually a complex, enigmatic, and wildly diverse phenomena. "Although science has made great advances in understanding the secrets of the Universe," says Libbrecht, "there remains a bit of mystery still in these remarkable ice structures."[2]

Snowflakes are typically created when water vapor freezes directly into a solid, entirely bypassing the liquid phase. By contrast, when *liquid* water freezes into a solid, it produces sleet—a very different beast than snow.

The appearance of a snowflake created inside a cloud is dictated primarily by the cloud's temperature and humidity. At relatively high or low temperatures (around -5°C/23°F or -30°C/-22°F, respectively), snowflakes precipitate out looking like six-sided hockey pucks, tubes, and needles.

Only at in-between temperatures (around -15°C/5°F) and relatively high humidity does a cloud produce the spectacular six-armed, starlike snowflakes everyone knows and loves. The kind that prompted Henry David Thoreau to exclaim: "How full of creative genius is the air in which these are generated! I should hardly admire more if real stars fell and lodged on my coat."[3]

Even though these stellar beauties look perfectly symmetrical, they aren't. During a snowflake's long, cloud-to-ground journey, its shape is distorted by random gusts of wind, wild swings in temperature and humidity, and collisions with dust particles, sleet, and other snowflakes.

For those same reasons, no two snowflakes are ever exactly alike.

Under very controlled lab conditions, Libbrecht has successfully grown pairs of snowflakes that look identical to the eye—and he made the news because of it—but, alas, upon really close inspection, even those were not exactly the same.

REFLECTION

There is no other person on the planet exactly like you. Sure, you might find others who *look* like you—there are websites devoted to finding your doppelgänger (www.twinstrangers.net)—but look-alikes aren't *you*. They don't even have your fingerprints.

Like snowflakes, we are all different. For one thing, our appearances are all over the map: We come in all shapes, sizes, and colors.

But more than that, the Bible explains that God equips each of us with a unique set of gifts; gifts that are matched to our one-of-a-kind purpose in life, our unique destiny.

And that's still not all.

We are different because our journeys in life are different. Some people are born with the proverbial silver spoon in their mouth. Others are born with enormous physical, mental, and emotional setbacks.

Yet, despite our many differences, God loves us all equally. Why? Because just as all snowflakes are different yet made of the same thing—water—we are all different yet made with God's Spirit.

That is what makes us all the same, but also truly unique.

THE CREATOR SPEAKS

You made all the delicate, inner parts of my body
and knit me together in my mother's womb.
Thank you for making me so wonderfully complex!
Your workmanship is marvelous—how well I know it.
PSALM 139:13-14

Life after Death

On the morning of May 18, 1980, deep within the bowels of Mount St. Helens, subterranean reservoirs of superheated water exploded with a thunderous boom heard miles away.

The eruption blew off the volcano's top twelve hundred feet, propelling in all directions an 800°F, 200 mph wind of sand grains and boulders as big as cars.

In a matter of minutes, this hellish *rock wind* leveled 150 square miles of the surrounding region and smothered a much larger area—*22,000 square miles*—in ash. Along the way, it snapped in half legions of 180-foot-tall pines, as though they were mere twigs, and seared and sandblasted the bark off countless other trees.

On the heels of the rock wind, massive mudflows created by a mixture of melted snow, rock, pumice, ash, and dirt barreled down the volcano's steep slopes. The dense sludge tore apart bridges, leveled houses, and inundated a total of 255 square miles, destroying and greatly disfiguring the landscape.

When it was all over, fifty-seven people were found dead. The afflicted region—dubbed the Pumice Plain—resembled the surface of the moon, covered over by a hardened layer of ash. It was totally lifeless: no plants, animals, organic matter, insects, or even microbes.

In 1982, however—just two years after the calamity—scientists were shocked to find a solo plant growing smack-dab in the middle of the Pumice Plain. It was a lupine (*Lupinus lepidus* var. *lobbii*), a low-growing herbaceous shrub, which very quickly began infusing the devastated soil with desperately needed nitrogen and organic matter.

Because of that single heroic lupine plant and the seedlings that sprouted all around it, the Pumice Plain began to recover miraculously fast. By 2007, the area—once a barren moonscape—was home to seventy-eight distinct plant species. By 2013, there were 137. And by 2016, the number had grown to *155*!

REFLECTION

Very few people will go through life without experiencing something that resembles a volcanic eruption. The rock winds of adversity and mudslides of misfortune leave you feeling devastated, wondering whether—and doubting that—you can ever recover.

Maybe you've lost a spouse early in life, or a child. Or perhaps you've been diagnosed with a terminal illness. Or you've gone bankrupt.

Your life suddenly looks like the Pumice Plain, like the bleak surface of the moon. What do you do now?

You can give into the calamity, totally surrendering to it. Or you can find something in the midst of the desolation for which you can be thankful.

All it takes is one small thing—like the little, lone lupine plant in the aftermath of Mount St. Helens' wrath. A friend or relative who has always been there for you, through thick and thin. Or, best of all, God, the very fountainhead of life and hope.

God has the power to transform your Pumice Plain into a garden. He demonstrated that power unmistakably by resurrecting the crucified Jesus.

No situation you'll ever face in life is too deathly for God to heal. From the volcanic ashes of your direst circumstances he is always able to bring forth new life—if only you'll let him.

THE CREATOR SPEAKS

And the one sitting on the throne said, "Look, I am making everything new! . . . Write this down, for what I tell you is trustworthy and true."

REVELATION 21:5

Poisonous Pleasures

Poison ivy (*Toxicodendron radicans*), a three-leaved plant native to Asia and North America, doesn't look poisonous at all. Yet every year, fifty million Americans find out the hard way that if you even just brush against it, your skin will erupt in an itchy, painful rash.

Why is that? Because unlike ordinary ivy, poison ivy has leaves that are infused with a toxic oil called urushiol, so absorbent it'll seep into your skin within minutes.

Being an oil, urushiol is also sticky and doesn't readily evaporate. So if it gets on your skin, clothes, shoes, camping gear, gloves, or tools, it can remain there, active, for up to *five years*.

Your only protection from being infected is to wash the oil off immediately with soap and water. But it's hard to do that completely because it only takes one billionth of a gram of urushiol to produce a rash, and the average accidental exposure is a hundred times that much.

Scientists estimate that 85 percent of humanity is susceptible to urushiol's toxicity. Incredibly, though, the other 15 percent can absorb large amounts of the oil into their skin without any adverse effects whatsoever.

But that remarkable immunity comes with a huge caveat. After several exposures, even people who've been resistant to poison ivy all their lives can suddenly succumb to its toxicity.

So, whichever camp you belong to, be sure to heed the old folk warning against poison ivy: "Leaves of three? Leave them be!"

REFLECTION

Day in and day out, you constantly face attractive or seemingly benign temptations that turn out to be extremely toxic. A sweet-tasting cocktail, a photo of a beautiful fashion model, an over-the-counter sleeping aid: After too many exposures to these seemingly harmless pleasures, even the most straitlaced person can ultimately fall victim to alcoholism, pornography, or drug addiction.

Once you're infected, it's not easy to scrub yourself clean. It takes something far more powerful than soap and water to do the job.

Expensive rehab clinics, psychotherapy, medical treatments—even they don't always work, especially if the infection is in part genetically driven. We now know, for example, that some people are born with a genetic predisposition to alcoholism.

According to the Bible, the very best way to battle temptation is to recognize it and avoid it in the first place. If that doesn't work—if you fall prey to the lure of sin—you're still not doomed.

God is ready, willing, and able to help wash you clean. Incredibly, cleaner even than you were before the awful encounter.

THE CREATOR SPEAKS

Though your sins are like scarlet,
  I will make them as white as snow.
Though they are red like crimson,
  I will make them as white as wool.
ISAIAH 1:18

169

Initial Conditions

According to classical physics, all we need to know in order to predict the entire future of anything are its "initial conditions." This means two things.

First, it means we need to know the object's present location in three-dimensional space. For any earthling, that's longitude, latitude, and altitude.

Second, it means we need to know the object's present velocity—which is *speed* plus *direction*.

For instance, the velocity of a steady wind might be thirty miles per hour in an easterly direction. Or the velocity of a car might be sixty miles per hour heading north.

In the 1700s, there were scientists who claimed they could predict people's futures simply by knowing their initial conditions. One such scientist was the Frenchman Pierre-Simon de Laplace.

Laplace imagined an all-knowing entity—which became known as Laplace's Demon—that knew the initial conditions of every single object in the universe.

For such an intellect, Laplace declared, "nothing would be uncertain and the future, as the past, would be present to its eyes."[1]

Laplace never delivered on his extravagant claim, and for good reason. In the 1920s, the old notions of a deterministic cosmos and Laplace's all-knowing Demon were replaced by the radically new quantum mechanical notions of a *probabilistic* cosmos and Heisenberg's uncertainty principle.

Because of that, we now understand two inconvenient truths: (1) It will always be impossible to know an object's initial conditions with any certainty; and (2) it will always be impossible to predict the future for anything or anyone with any certainty.

REFLECTION

For better or worse, you and I have free will. God has made us autonomous creatures.

This means that God doesn't dictate our every move. He's not some Svengali pulling our strings. Nevertheless, he already knows every decision we will ever make in life—including those that will bring him great joy, and those that will break his heart.

How is God able to know our futures so precisely, in defiance of the quantum mechanical laws of uncertainty? Well, because he created the universe which means he exists outside of it, outside ordinary space and time. For him, past, present, and future do not happen sequentially; they exist *simultaneously*.

Put another way, God knows everything that has happened, is happening, and will ever happen to you. He even knows the decision you're about to make concerning this passage—whether you'll shrug it off or let it sink in.

So be sure to choose wisely. Be sure your decision doesn't break God's heart.

THE CREATOR SPEAKS

Today I have given you the choice between life and death,
between blessings and curses. Now I call on heaven and earth
to witness the choice you make. Oh, that you would choose life,
so that you and your descendants might live!
DEUTERONOMY 30:19

Colorful Characters

Contrary to popular belief, chameleons (family Chamaeleonidae) do not change color in order to blend into the background. They do so, scientists have discovered, primarily to regulate their body temperature and—ironically—to stand out in certain, important situations.

Chameleons have special, multilayered, iridescent skin cells called *iridophores*, which act like reflective prisms. By either relaxing or exciting these cells—thus altering their relative placement, orientation, and density on the skin—chameleons can turn themselves into a veritable kaleidoscope of colors.

These lizards are cold-blooded creatures, so they're at the constant mercy of surrounding temperature fluctuations. That's where their color-changing ability comes in very handy.

In hot weather, chameleons clothe themselves in light colors, which reflect sunlight. In cold weather, they change into something darker—usually a dark brown—the better to absorb the warming sunlight.

Chameleons also change outfits to look flashier to the opposite sex. A female common chameleon (*Chamaeleo chamaeleon*) looking for action changes into a suit with bright yellow spots. A female uninterested in mating will wear something with low-key blue and yellow spots—a universal Do Not Disturb sign warning males to stay away.

Male chameleons looking for action dress flamboyantly—not just to attract females, but to outcompete other males. They'll put on the brightest, boldest, most dazzling colors and patterns their iridophores can muster, hoping females will notice and choose *them* for mating.

REFLECTION

We all know people who are colorful characters. They're typically the life of any party, boisterous, with bigger-than-normal personalities and a seemingly limitless repertoire of entertaining stories.

Some colorful characters are genuinely joy-filled, others are not. Their outsized personalities mask serious, inner insecurities, like chameleons putting on a dazzling show that's only skin deep.

The Bible invites you to be a deep person, which doesn't mean you can't have fun. It means you're always *yourself*, wherever you go; you don't hide behind phony facades just to impress others.

There's a beauty to being yourself, whether you're a genuinely colorful character or a person who enjoys helping out behind the scenes, well away from the limelight.

In one way or another, authentic behavior serves you well and enriches all our lives. Above all, authentic behavior, colorful or not, catches God's eye . . . and wins his approval.

THE CREATOR SPEAKS

Hypocrites! For you are like whitewashed tombs which indeed appear beautiful outwardly, but inside are full of dead men's bones and all uncleanness.
MATTHEW 23:27, NKJV

Your Divine Purpose

Every year in the semiarid deserts of the American Southwest, Mexico, and elsewhere, scores of small, whitish moths flit industriously from one yucca plant to another. They are all in a big hurry because they have a very, very short time in which to fulfill their singular purpose in life.

Yucca moths (*Tegeticula yuccasella*) begin their brief, days-long existence when they emerge from underground cocoons in early spring, precisely when the yucca plants are starting to flower. They don't have tongues, because their short life span doesn't require them to eat anything.

Very quickly, the males and females pair up and mate. Once that's done, the males die off.

The fertilized females immediately go to work collecting grains of yucca pollen, gathering them into tiny balls under their chins, as if they were making snowballs. A typical pollen ball is three times bigger than the female's head!

Each pregnant female then flies off in search of a yucca flower for two purposes: a safe place to lay her eggs, and to use her outsized pollen ball to fertilize the flower. Once that's done, she promptly dies.

Days later, the yucca moth eggs hatch and the fertilized yucca flowers produce fruits and seeds, providing the newborn caterpillars with shelter and food. By the end of the flowering season, all the yucca caterpillars have dropped to the ground, burrowed down a few inches, and safely cocooned themselves.

The following spring, legions of newly metamorphosed yucca moths come out of hiding, take to the air, and repeat the life cycle of their parents. With only a few days to accomplish their purpose, they rush to fulfill their species' small, sacrificial role in keeping our beloved planet alive and well.

REFLECTION

Like the yucca moth, you have a divine purpose. God knit you in a precise way, just so you can fulfill that important destiny. There's no one like you. There *never has been* anyone like you. There *never will be* anyone like you.

Dwelling within every subatomic particle of every cell of your body is a mysterious spirit that connects you with your creator. If you make good use of that connection—if, in the Sturm und Drang of life, you silence yourself and listen for God's still, small, loving voice speaking to you—then, like a yucca moth, you will find and fulfill your divine purpose.

It's a purpose that will bless not only you, but also God's entire creation.

THE CREATOR SPEAKS

Be still, and know that I am God!
PSALM 46:10

For I know the plans I have for you.... They are plans for good and not for disaster, to give you a future and a hope.
JEREMIAH 29:11

The Voice

Sperm whales (*Physeter macrocephalus*) are superlative in at least four ways.

First, they are the largest, heaviest, toothed mammals in the world. Mature females are about thirty-five feet long and weigh about fifteen tons; males can grow to fifty-two feet long and typically weigh forty-five tons.

Second, sperm whales inhabit every ocean on the planet Earth. They range from just short of the Arctic Circle (60° N) to just short of the Antarctic Circle (60° S); and from ocean surfaces to ocean depths of more than 10,000 feet.

Third, sperm whales—carnivores who love to eat giant squid, sharks, and other fish—consume up to 3.5 percent of their body weight daily—that's up to a half ton for a mature female, one-and-a-half tons for a mature male.

Fourth, a sperm whale's monstrous, ten-ton head houses a waxlike lens that focuses the whale's powerful voice like a laser beam. The whale emits a slow series of clicks to navigate in dark, deep water, and a rapid series of clicks—like bats—to locate and zero in on prey.

Male sperm whales *trumpet* their arrival in feeding grounds, much as elephants do. And they send out *codas*—coded sequences of three to twenty clicks lasting up to two seconds.

Sperm whales can tell if a stranger belongs to their family or clan of families by its *dialect*. That is, by exactly how the stranger pronounces its codas.

REFLECTION

A sperm whale's voice is powerful enough to shatter your eardrums. God's voice is infinitely more powerful than that—yet it *doesn't* shatter your eardrums.

Yes, that doesn't make sense—it's downright illogical—yet it's anything but nonsense. It's *translogical*.

According to the Bible, God's voice is powerful enough to have spoken an entire universe into being. Yet gentle enough to be described in the King James Bible as "a still small voice."[1]

Learn, then, from God.

When you want to get people's attention, don't shout. That'll only make them cover their ears and tune you out, as if a nearby sperm whale bull were trumpeting at them.

Instead, try whispering. More likely than not, it'll get their attention and cause them to lean in and listen to what you have to say.

That is truly a powerful voice.

THE CREATOR SPEAKS

> The LORD passed by, and a mighty windstorm hit the mountain . . . but the LORD was not in the wind. After the wind there was an earthquake, but the LORD was not in the earthquake. And after the earthquake there was a fire, but the LORD was not in the fire. And after the fire there was the sound of a gentle whisper.
>
> 1 KINGS 19:11-12

> The voice of the LORD is powerful;
>   The voice of the LORD is full of majesty.
>
> PSALM 29:4, ESV

Bless Your Heart

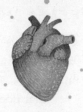

In the second century AD, the famous Greek physician and philosopher Galen proposed an incorrect theory about blood circulation that went on to dominate medical science for some 1,500 years. His main thesis was that blood is continuously created by the liver and continuously consumed by body tissue.

Galen's misguided idea led to the common and dangerous practice of bloodletting. Well into the 1800s, European physicians treated sick patients by cutting them and letting their blood drain out, or by applying blood-sucking leeches—believing their livers would promptly replace the supposedly diseased blood with fresh, healthy blood.

In 1628 William Harvey—British physician to King James I—wrote *Anatomical Studies on the Motion of the Heart and Blood in Animals*. In it he offered a theory radically different from Galen's. Blood is not constantly created and consumed, he explained; rather, it is recycled over and over again by the heart.

Despite his impeccable scientific credentials, Harvey was brutally mocked by the pro-Galen scientific consensus of the day and consequently lost much of his private practice. Today, we would say he was *canceled*.

Later in life, he became something of a recluse, lamenting: "Much better is it oftentimes to grow wise at home and in private, than by publishing what you have amassed with infinite labour, to stir up tempests that may rob you of peace and quiet for the rest of your days."[1]

Harvey was ultimately vindicated, and today we understand just how truly amazing the human heart is. Every day it beats about 115,000 times, pumping about 2,000 gallons of blood.

That means, from birth to death, your heart beats an average of *three billion* times, without once taking a break.

REFLECTION

We are a people intoxicated by our scientific and technological prowess, who believe we can improve nature, God's creation—or at least, duplicate it at will.

Despite decades of intense effort, however, we have not come close to duplicating the human heart. Even our cleverest inventions are clunky pumps made of plastic and metal, driven by machines outside the body.

One of the best is the Aeson artificial heart made by a French company called Carmat; yet, even it is ridiculously primitive. The implanted portion of the device, about the size of a real human heart, is made of plastic and cow heart tissue. It weighs more than ten times what a normal human heart does.

The Aeson mechanical heart is connected by a thick tube that passes through the chest wall to a heavy bag slung on the patient's shoulder. The bag contains the battery-powered motors and hydraulic fluid that drive the contraption. The rechargeable lithium batteries are good for just four hours before needing to be plugged in and recharged.

This artificial heart is designed for temporary usage. It's for patients with severe heart disease who are expecting a real human heart transplant within 180 days.[2]

Think about that next time you hear someone talking trash about God and crowing about what we humans can do by ourselves.

THE CREATOR SPEAKS

"My thoughts are nothing like your thoughts," says the LORD.
"And my ways are far beyond anything you could imagine.
For just as the heavens are higher than the earth,
*   so my ways are higher than your ways*
*   and my thoughts higher than your thoughts."*
ISAIAH 55:8-9

Common Scents

Plants and animals were using wireless communication long before we humans invented radio, television, and cell phones. But we didn't know it until the mid-twentieth century.

Our awakening began in the late 1800s, when scientists noticed that a newly born female silkworm moth attracted the frenzied attention of scores of male moths from near and far. French naturalist Jean-Henri Fabre, speculated that the male suitors were being triggered by an invisible love potion given off by the virgin female—some kind of "effluvia of extreme subtlety."

In 1959 German biochemist Adolf Butenandt discovered that the love potion was, in fact, a cocktail of chemicals we now call pheromones. He and his team spent twenty years milking a few milligrams of the powerful aphrodisiac from 500,000 female silkworm moths (*Bombyx mori*). He named it *bombykol*.

Today, scientists realize that animals of every description communicate wirelessly using pheromones. From ants, wasps, and mice to salamanders, lobsters, and elephants. In each case, pheromones trigger significant changes in an individual's behavior and development.

A sex-hungry boar gives off a pheromone (5-α-Androst-16-en-3-one) that causes any nearby sow in heat to instantly freeze and surrender to him.

A new mother rabbit gives off a pheromone (2-Methylbut-2-enal) that triggers her babies' suckling behavior.

A wounded bee gives off a pheromone (e.g., isopentyl acetate) that alerts its hive-mates to a clear and present danger.

All in all, if you could hear what these legions of different organisms can smell, the unrelenting cacophony would be deafening.

REFLECTION

Science has discovered that our brains are especially good at processing visual information. That's why today's most popular social media platforms—YouTube, Instagram, TikTok, Facebook—all rely on the power of photos and videos.

Knowing our brain's affinity for visual information, God sends us visions—wirelessly. It's his equivalent, if you will, of the internet.

Today and every day, therefore, *stay alert to God's wireless communications*! Spend less time on social media and more time watching out for all that God has to show you.

THE CREATOR SPEAKS

> *This vision is for a future time....*
> *If it seems slow in coming, wait patiently,*
> *for it will surely take place.*
> *It will not be delayed.*
> HABAKKUK 2:3

Unquenchable Love

At roughly 2 a.m. on January 23, 1973, the good people of Heimaey, Iceland, were jolted awake by the surprising eruption of Helgafell (holy mountain), the island's long-dormant volcano. Young Kristján H. Kristjánsson reacted with a mixture of horror and awe: "When I looked out of the window, I saw a volcanic eruption close to my home. It was a very dramatic and beautiful sight."[1]

All 5,300 Heimaey residents rushed down to the village's sole harbor, clambered onto several dozen fishing boats, and hightailed it to Iceland's main island—all within six hours. Helgafell itself not only kept erupting—its lava incinerating parts of the village and threatening to destroy the harbor—but it also spawned a second volcano, called Eldfell (fire mountain).

But the people of Heimaey didn't give up. Determined to rescue their village and its all-important fishing port, they brought in huge pumps and hoses and began dousing the advancing wall of red-hot lava with ice-cold North Atlantic seawater.

After pummeling the massive lava flow for many weeks with some 1.6 *billion* gallons of seawater, the residents of Heimaey made history. They stopped the lava flow dead in its tracks and saved their precious harbor.

On July 3, the residents declared the eruption to be over. Then they proceeded to fully restore their island home—which, much to their delight, now had about ten percent more landmass than before, thanks to the solidification of the sprawling lava beds created by Helgafell and Eldfell.

Kristjánsson says he'll never forget watching the process unfold. "We sailed through a narrow path between a high cliff and glowing lava entering the ocean. . . . I found it humbling and scaring to be so close to the creation of new land by the Great Architect of the Universe."[2]

REFLECTION

According to the Bible, everything about God is both beautiful and terrifying. That includes his love for you.

His love is beautiful because it's unconditional. He loves you just as you are, warts and all, and he desires for you to love him in return.

But it's also terrifying because it puts you in his debt. That's one of the unavoidable, awesome consequences of being on the receiving end of unconditional love.

Many people don't like being in debt to anyone, least of all God. So they react to it the way Heimaey's residents reacted to Helgafell's beautiful and terrifying eruption: They flee from it, then fight it off with everything they have.

The choice, therefore, is both clear and consequential. Fight to preserve your selfish, willful tendencies; or surrender to God's beautiful and terrifying love.

THE CREATOR SPEAKS

Love flashes like fire,
the brightest kind of flame.
Many waters cannot quench love,
nor can rivers drown it.
SONG OF SONGS 8:6-7

The Tiniest Thing Matters

Universes have personalities, just like people, and they fall roughly into three categories: stoic, composed, and volatile.

In a stoic universe, events have little or no consequences. Even when something dramatic happens, the universe remains stone-faced; it doesn't react very much, or at all.

In a composed universe, events have proportionate consequences. The universe reacts in small ways to small provocations and in big ways to big ones; the reaction is always measured.

In a volatile universe, events have outsized consequences. At even the tiniest irritation, the universe blows up. It behaves as if it's high on caffeine.

Scientists as far back as Aristotle believed that our universe was composed. Using today's lingo, they believed the universe to be *linear*—that cause and effect are always in line with each other.

In the 1970s, this ancient worldview was overturned by the work of a little-known MIT meteorologist named Edward Lorenz. While studying the behavior of weather, Lorenz stumbled upon an astonishing truth: We live not in a composed, linear universe, but in a highly volatile, nonlinear one.

Lorenz used the term *chaos* to describe the explosiveness of our world. One especially popular concept born of chaos theory is known as the *butterfly effect*.

According to Lorenz's chaos theory—i.e., the butterfly effect—the mere flapping of a butterfly's tiny wings in Brazil is enough to trigger a chain reaction in the atmosphere that ends up as a devastating thunderstorm in Texas.

REFLECTION

Think about what life would be like if God had created a *stoic* universe. Nothing for us would ever change. Hoping for a better day would be pointless. The very concept of hope wouldn't even exist.

Think about what life would be like if God had created a *composed* universe. There would never be any surprises. Worse, you wouldn't matter in the great scheme of things, because in a composed universe significance is always reckoned in proportion to size.

Perhaps now you can see why God decided to create a *volatile* universe. In a *volatile* universe, unexpected things always happen. A small shepherd boy can become a powerful king. A stuttering outlaw can become a legendary emancipator of slaves. A poor kid from the Mexican barrios of East Los Angeles can grow up to teach at Harvard and write best-selling books.

It's the only kind of universe where hope exists, and is validated every day in a million different and spectacular ways. It's a universe where miracles can happen, and always do. A universe, above all, where you—yes, *you*—are unimaginably important, no matter where you come from or how many bad choices you've made in life.

THE CREATOR SPEAKS

> No eye has seen, no ear has heard,
>   and no mind has imagined
> what God has prepared
>   for those who love him.
>
> 1 CORINTHIANS 2:9

Healing from the Inside Out

Chinese giant salamanders (*Andrias davidianus*) are almost six feet long, weigh more than one hundred pounds, and usually live for up to fifty years—with some notable exceptions. In 2015, researchers discovered one Chinese giant salamander that was an estimated two hundred years old!

These giant amphibians spend some time on land, but mostly they stay in the lakes and mountain rivers of Central China. On land, they breathe using lungs; but underwater they breathe in a very unusual way—through their *skin*, not through gills.

The salamander's skin is uniquely porous, to allow in oxygen but not water. Once through the skin, the oxygen is absorbed via osmosis directly into the salamander's bloodstream.

If a salamander is injured, its remarkable skin oozes out a slimy, protein-rich white fluid. Almost like magic, this mucosal fluid helps seal and heal the wound.

Scientists who study the healing properties of this mucosal fluid have discovered it works like an exceptional medical adhesive. One day, they predict, doctors everywhere will routinely use it—or something like it—to seal deep cuts without having to use stitches.

Chinese doctors have been using the salamander's miraculous skin secretions for more than a thousand years to heal serious burns.

REFLECTION

Modern scientific medicine enables us to treat and heal many afflictions. But it cannot heal a broken heart—or, worse, a wounded soul or broken spirit.

Treating the outward symptoms—sadness, loneliness, depression, hopelessness—does nothing to cure the root cause. According to the Bible, the only way to do that is from the *inside out*.

The good news is that the human spirit is uniquely porous, to allow God's Spirit in. Invite him into your life, and he will begin ministering to your ailing heart, soul, and human spirit.

And that's not just the Bible talking. Scientists have studied and affirmed the efficacy of God's Spirit—even though they don't call it that. In thousands of studies, people who take God seriously—who attend church regularly and pray—heal faster after surgery, need fewer pain medications, and are generally more joyful than people who don't.

They also live longer. In one study of Black Americans, the increase in longevity was a whopping *fourteen years!*[1]

THE CREATOR SPEAKS

> Let all that I am praise the LORD;
>> may I never forget the good things he does for me.
> He forgives all my sins
>> and heals all my diseases.

PSALM 103:2-3

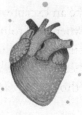

Shelter from the Storm

Tornadoes are generally considered the deadliest storms on Earth. Every year, in the United States alone—where about 70 percent of these lethal tempests happen—more than 1,200 tornadoes kill roughly eighty people, hurt many more, and cause billions of dollars in property damage.

Most US tornadoes rip through a narrow corridor called Tornado Alley, which includes much of northern Texas, Oklahoma, Kansas, Missouri, and parts of Louisiana, Iowa, Nebraska, and eastern Colorado.[1]

The deadliest tornadoes sprout from severe thunderstorms called *supercells*, when—by a mechanism that scientists still don't fully understand—surface winds gather themselves into a horizontal, rotating cylinder. At some fateful point, the supercell's strong updrafts stand the rotating cylinder on end, creating a recognizable tornado.

At that point, the twister can spin up to 250 miles per hour and charge forward at up to 300 miles per hour. As it does so, it tears through everything in its path like a precision buzzsaw. People and property not precisely in its track remain untouched.

Adding to a tornado's deadliness is its unpredictability. Unlike other natural disasters such as hurricanes, mudslides, and volcanoes, we find it difficult or impossible to know when a tornado will form, notwithstanding the help of real-time, supercomputer modeling.

Even when we spot well-known warning signs, there's only a 50/50 chance a tornado will actually develop. Real-time intelligence reports from so-called storm chasers—volunteers and professionals who drive around scouring the sky for signs of a tornado—do help; but even they cannot guess where exactly a sudden tornado will head off and wreak havoc.

People's best hope for surviving a tornado is to take shelter. The National Severe Storms Lab (NSSL), based in Norman, Oklahoma—smack in the middle of Tornado Alley—offers plans online for building in-house safe rooms. "A safe room is a hardened structure," the NSSL's website explains, "specifically designed to . . . provide near-absolute protection in extreme wind events, including tornadoes and hurricanes."[2]

REFLECTION

Even when everything in your life is hunky-dory, every new day holds the potential of unleashing a tornado in your life. In the blink of an eye, without any warning, your world can be utterly shattered.

When that happens, it's too late to scramble into a safe room. Besides, what kind of man-made shelter can save you from a random auto collision, a heart attack, or a drive-by shooting?

In such times, God—who is stronger than any NSSL-approved, steel-reinforced concrete structure—is the only safe place you can count on. When a tornado upends your life, God's arms—wrapped securely around you—are the only thing in the universe that can help you recover, rebuild, and resume life with genuine hope for sunny skies again.

THE CREATOR SPEAKS

God is our refuge and strength,
   always ready to help in times of trouble.
So we will not fear when earthquakes come
   and the mountains crumble into the sea.
Let the oceans roar and foam.
   Let the mountains tremble as the waters surge!

PSALM 46:1-3

Bigger than You

The Great Barrier Reef—the largest living structure on Earth—is one of the Seven Natural Wonders of the World. Comprised of 2,900 individual reefs and 900 islands, it spans 130,000 square miles—big enough to be seen with the naked eye from the moon!

The Great Barrier Reef's skeleton is made of calcium carbonate, the rock-hard substance in eggshells and pearls. It's been created over many, many years by billions of polyps, creatures related to jellyfish and anemones and no bigger than a grain of sand. Decorating the hard skeleton, like so many tiny shrubs, are a wide variety of soft corals.

Altogether, the Great Barrier Reef is a magnificent kaleidoscope of 600 kinds of coral, with wonderful names such as the organ pipe coral (*Tubipora musica*), smooth cauliflower coral (*Stylophora pistillata*), and finger coral (*Montipora digitata*). It's also home to some thirty species of whales, dolphins, and porpoises; six species of sea turtles; 215 species of birds; and 1,500 fish species.

The Great Barrier Reef is a dazzling metropolis pulsing with life day and night. A remarkable study in how wildly diverse organisms can live together in perfect harmony.

REFLECTION

We humans are social creatures; we don't like being alone, which is why we place recalcitrant prisoners in solitary confinement. But our being social creatures spells both good news and bad news.

First, the bad news.

Our sociability brings us together, but our conflicting agendas inevitably create disagreements. Disagreements steadily tear away at whatever unity we might've had, until it all falls apart.

But there is good news, as well.

On those wonderful occasions when we all band together for a common cause, we're able to achieve monumental results—results no person working alone could possibly accomplish.

We see this all the time in construction. People with vastly different backgrounds—from college-trained architects to wealthy investors to middle-class vendors to blue-collar workers—all come together to build something spectacular, like the Taj Mahal, the Brooklyn Bridge, or the Notre Dame Cathedral—structures that require multiple generations and disciplines to complete.

Next time you come together with others for a common purpose, great or small, call to mind the example of the Great Barrier Reef. Set aside your ego and your differences with other group members, and work hard for unity, so that you can increase the odds of being part of something truly magnificent and long-lasting.

THE CREATOR SPEAKS

A kingdom divided by civil war will collapse. Similarly, a family splintered by feuding will fall apart.
MARK 3:24-25

I appeal to you, dear brothers and sisters . . . live in harmony with each other. Let there be no divisions. . . . Rather, be of one mind, united in thought and purpose.
1 CORINTHIANS 1:10

Before You
Know It

Peregrine falcons (*Falco peregrinus*) are unmatched in at least two big ways. They are the fastest bird—actually, the fastest animal—in the world; and they're the most widely distributed bird of prey on the planet, inhabiting every continent except Antarctica, plus many island nations.

No wonder they're called *peregrine*. It means "having a tendency to wander," from the medieval Latin *peregrinus*, meaning "foreign" or "pilgrim."[1]

Peregrines primarily hunt birds and can spot a midsize one from a mile away. Once the prey is at a lower altitude and within range, a peregrine tucks in its wings; tightens its body—taking on the shape of a missile—and dives at more than two hundred miles per hour! That's more than three times faster than a cheetah in a full sprint and nine times faster than the world's fastest Olympic runner.

The peregrine's impact is usually enough to make the kill. But if not, it will use its strong talons and sharp beak to finish the job.

Peregrines are not picky eaters. They'll happily devour songbirds, ducks, shorebirds, and other birds of prey—including hawks, eagles, and other falcons.

They even like pigeons. In fact, peregrines often thrive in urban areas, joyfully dive-bombing plump pigeons amid the glass-and-steel skyscrapers of the city, high above the noisy street traffic. These superlative birds also like nesting on the ledges of tall buildings, safely out of human reach.

REFLECTION

According to the Bible, Satan behaves very much like a fierce bird of prey. He lies in wait, then from out of nowhere strikes with lightning speed.

Before realizing you've been attacked, you're in Satan's viselike grip. Alone, you stand no chance against such a skillful predator.

For want of a better word, you need a supernatural *bodyguard* at your side at all times. Actually, not just at your side, but all around you.

That, the Bible explains, is precisely what God offers you: 360-degree, 24/7/365 protection. It won't entirely save you from being dive-bombed—Ephesians 6:10-18 warns you must keep your "heavenly armor" on—but it will shield you from succumbing to Satan's evil intentions.

Many people today consider themselves too sophisticated to believe in Satan—an actual being who is the wellspring of all malevolence. They're like city pigeons living fat and happy off the crumbs of secular society—until that one unexpected moment when a dark shadow swoops down out of nowhere and violently impacts their lives.

Don't be a pigeon, my friend. Just because you don't believe in the reality of Satan doesn't mean he doesn't exist.

THE CREATOR SPEAKS

Nothing can ever separate us from God's love. . . . No power in the sky above or in the earth below—indeed, nothing in all creation will ever be able to separate us from the love of God that is revealed in Christ Jesus our Lord.
ROMANS 8:38-39

True Colors

All the stars that twinkle in the night sky appear to be white. But look more carefully, as astronomers do, and you'll discover that stars come in every visible color of the rainbow and beyond.

That vibrant reality has enormous importance to astronomers. Why? Because astronomers can deduce a great deal about a star just by knowing its true colors.

For example, the color of a star tells us its temperature. Just look at the flames on an ordinary gas range: Blue flames are hotter than orange-red ones.

The color of a star also tells us its age. Young stars tend to be blue because they burn hot and bright. Aging stars turn reddish-orange as they lose their fire. Our own sun—which now shines a bright yellow—will one day become a worn-out, bloated red giant.

The color of a star also tells us a lot about its chemical makeup. That's because each chemical element has its own unique color fingerprint.

Finally, the color of a star can tell us if it's moving away or toward Earth. It's like being able to tell if an ambulance is moving away or toward you, by listening to the sound of its siren. If the siren's pitch decreases, it's moving away, and vice versa. It's called the Doppler effect.

Likewise, if a star is moving toward us, its true colors will be shifted toward the blue end of the rainbow. If a star is moving away from us, its true colors will be shifted toward the red end.

Imagine! If stars weren't so colorful, we'd know much less about the heavens than we do. As British astronomer Sir William Bragg once declared: "Light brings us the news of the Universe."[1]

REFLECTION

The words in the Bible, like the colors of starlight, open our eyes to heavenly truths. This is one of them: Sizing up someone's true colors tells you a lot about them.

The Jewish priests of Jesus' day appeared to be devout and sincere. But Jesus looked past appearances and saw their true colors. Most of them were hypocrites, and he called them out for it.

What are your true colors?

Are you authentic or a fraud? Do you practice what you preach? Or do you just talk a good game?

You might fool others, but God sees right through all the subterfuge, all the window dressing. He sees the real you. He sees your heart.

So stop pretending to be someone you're not. Starting today, step out of the shadows of deception and shine brightly and truly, just like the stars above.

THE CREATOR SPEAKS

Those who are wise will shine as bright as the sky, and those who lead many to righteousness will shine like the stars forever.
DANIEL 12:3

Let your light shine before others, so that they may see your good works and give glory to your Father who is in heaven.
MATTHEW 5:16, ESV

Pint-Sized Powerhouse

Cacao trees (*Theobroma cacao*) grow up to forty feet tall and produce seeds whose chocolaty goodness people worldwide crave and spend roughly $1 trillion annually to consume. Yet, incredibly, every one of these prized trees and the entire chocolate industry depend on a minuscule insect called the chocolate midge fly (family Ceratopogonidae).

The reason for the tiny insect's outsized importance is simple: It's the only pollinator in the world small enough and skilled enough to navigate its way into the cacao tree's tiny, twisted flowers. With yellowish petals and pink sepals, the problematic flowers grow only on the cacao's trunk and largest branches—a phenomenon scientists call cauliflory.

Even under ideal circumstances, chocolate midges themselves have a tough time pollinating the cacao's tricky flowers. The insects' success rate is further sabotaged by the fact that many commercial cacao trees are now grown on sun-drenched plantations, a far cry from the heavily shaded rain forests that wild cacaos and their all-important midget pollinators call home.

On top of all that, the aroma of cultivated cacao flowers doesn't have the same attraction to the chocolate midges as their native counterparts. Scientists estimate that a cacao wildflower has roughly seventy-five distinct fragrances, whereas a domesticated cacao flower has only a few.

All these formidable obstacles, and others, add up to a pretty dismal success rate. On average the industrious, dexterous chocolate midges successfully pollinate a mere three out of every 1,000 cultivated cacao flowers.

REFLECTION

Experiencing joy in life is a lot like eating a box of exquisite, handcrafted chocolates—assuming, of course, you like chocolate. Each day, like each bite, is heavenly.

You might guess that such happiness comes most easily to people born into wealth, but that's not true. True joy in all its physical, emotional, and spiritual complexity usually comes from hard, meaningful work, making wise choices, and having a healthy frame of mind.

A healthy frame of mind. What does that mean exactly?

According to the Bible, it means having an attitude that radiates a positivity rooted in a strong, sincere faith in God. It's a winning attitude that requires you not just to *believe* in God, but to *trust God completely*; to expect him to come through for you, even if it isn't always in the way you expect or want.

In science, likewise, we know of many important phenomena that require certain preconditions to be satisfied. A fire doesn't happen unless three things come together at the same time and in the right way: fuel, oxygen, and a thermal trigger (e.g., a spark). Likewise, a cocoa bean doesn't happen unless a chocolate midge successfully infiltrates and pollinates a convoluted cacao flower.

That's what having a healthy frame of mind means. It means trusting God with everything you have.

Do that and you'll experience more true joy than eating a box of the best-tasting chocolates money can buy.

THE CREATOR SPEAKS

"You don't have enough faith," Jesus told them. "I tell you the truth, if you had faith even as small as a mustard seed, you could say to this mountain, 'Move from here to there,' and it would move. Nothing would be impossible."

MATTHEW 17:20

Bigger than Infinity

Over time, our idea of *big* has grown by leaps and bounds.

Ancient Greek philosophers considered the starry heavens big—as big as anything gets. Still, they believed it to be finite in size, capable of being fully understood by human reason.

They called this finite, orderly, knowable universe a *kosmos*, from which we get the English word *cosmos*—although, to today's astronomers, the cosmos is infinite in size.

In the late 1800s, German mathematician Georg Cantor took the idea of *big* a gigantic step further. He revealed the existence of *transfinite* quantities even bigger than infinity.

Bigger than infinity? Yes.

The smallest of Cantor's transfinite numbers—*aleph-null*—corresponds to the garden-variety infinity we all know and love. It's how big we believe the universe to be.

Beyond that is a sequence of ever-greater transfinite numbers—aleph-one, aleph-two, aleph-three, and so forth. There's no limit to the bigness of Cantor's numbers.

Transfinite numbers make the traditional concept of infinity seem laughably small. They also open our eyes to the possibility that something bigger than the universe actually exists.

REFLECTION

If you ask people how big they think God is, they'll usually say, *infinitely* big. But it's more complicated than that.

According to the Bible, the very concept of size doesn't apply to God because he's not a spatial being any more than he is a temporal one. Since God created space and time, he transcends them both.

Think of it this way: The *Mona Lisa*, whose entire cosmos is a flat, finite, 2D canvas, cannot possibly fathom Leonardo's—her creator's—4D space-time cosmos. Likewise, we cannot fathom God's transfinite, dimensionless cosmos.

Because he's dimensionless, there's no yardstick with which to size up God and his realm. Like Cantor's transfinite numbers, God is not just beyond comprehension, he is beyond the very notion of comprehension.

THE CREATOR SPEAKS

Behold, heaven and the highest heaven cannot contain you.
1 KINGS 8:27, ESV

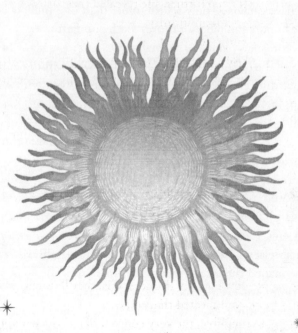

Beyond Comprehension

According to science's timetable, 540 million years ago, there was an unprecedented explosion of diverse, complex, fully developed life forms on Eath. The cause of this big bang of life—technically called the *Cambrian Explosion*—remains a deep, scientific mystery today.

Whatever caused it, the event was so fruitful we're not even close to fully itemizing the huge variety of different plants and animals it produced. Scientists have cataloged only a little more than one million of the estimated one hundred million (or more) species on Earth.

Discovering new plant and animal species isn't easy. Many of them live deep beneath the ocean, inside active volcanoes, or within dense forests.

Another difficulty is the cataloging process. Even with the help of DNA mapping, science has yet to concoct a perfect taxonomic system. A supposedly new species might turn out to be an old one, and vice versa.

Despite these challenges, however, we find and name thousands of newly discovered species every year. It seems the earth is a beautiful, endless cornucopia of surprises. In 2022 alone, we discovered two new kinds of scorpions (*Paruroctonus soda* and *Paruroctonus conclusus*); a new aquatic plant, Bolivia's giant water lily (*Victoria boliviana*); a seven-inch-long slug, Europe's giant keelback (*Limax pseudocinereoniger*); and a never-before-seen mammal living deep within the Brazilian Atlantic Forest: the maned three-toed sloth (*Bradypus crinitus*).

Sometimes we even discover *Lazarus taxa*—plants and animals thought to be extinct. Scientists believed the piglike Chacoan peccary (*Catagonus wagneri*) disappeared during the last ice age. But in the 1970s they found herds of them still living in South America.

Even more dramatic is the saga of the coelacanth (genus *Latimeria*), a fish with odd, footlike fins. Scientists claimed it went extinct *sixty-five million years* ago; but in 1938, one was found swimming in the waters of South Africa, and another one was found near Indonesia in 1998.

This news is especially stunning because the coelacanth is no small creature. It is six feet long and weighs two hundred pounds—yet, incredibly, it managed to remain hidden in plain sight for hundreds of years!

REFLECTION

I wrote this book to give you a glimpse of the boundless beauty that exists throughout the universe—whether you call it the natural world or God's creation. Not just way out in space or far beneath the ocean, but right under your nose. I wrote to open your eyes and ears—and *all* your senses—to the diversity and endless surprises that surround us and infuse us.

This book is an invitation to open your mind to the possibility that all of it—from the immortal jellyfish and wandering albatross to the jewel wasp and giant tubeworm—is not merely an accident, but the intentional creation of God who is beyond comprehension. A God who creates beauty because he values it. A God who designed you not just to eat, sleep, and procreate—as modern Darwinism would have it—but to value and create beauty, just as he does.

Above all, this book is an invitation for you to look past the obvious, past the humdrum routines of your everyday life; to look beyond the superficial and the all-too-pervasive ugliness of what we've done to God's creation. An invitation to behold the Creator who beckons us to experience the awe and wonder of his glorious masterpiece.

THE CREATOR SPEAKS

Have you never heard?
Have you never understood?
The LORD is the everlasting God,
the Creator of all the earth.
He never grows weak or weary.
No one can measure the depths of his understanding.

ISAIAH 40:28

Acknowledgments

Every book I've written was made possible by a small army of truly special people. This book is no exception.

Many thanks to Laurel, my smart, beautiful wife for her faithful support, keen eye, and superb judgment. I love you.

Thank you to Wes Yoder, my incomparable, highly respected, long-time agent whose indefatigable efforts made this book happen.

Thank you to Jan Long Harris, my wonderful, gracious, elegant publisher who helped immeasurably to inspire this work, and to encourage its execution—and to her legion of gifted colleagues at Tyndale.

Thank you to Dave Lindstedt, the most talented, enthusiastic, and enjoyable editor I've ever had the privilege of knowing. He and his crack team of editorial virtuosos are second to none.

Thank you to Maxfield Thompson, the hardworking, positive-minded, smart young man who helped identify and research many of the wonders of creation included in this book. It's been a joy to watch him rise to the challenge and grow.

Finally, thank you to my many loyal readers and fellow travelers worldwide. Their messages of love, support, and encouragement help keep me going and affirm the calling I feel from the brilliant, loving Creator to whom my life is fully and cheerfully dedicated.

Notes

INTRODUCTION
1. Romans 12:2.

INVITATION 4: RESILIENCE
1. Job 2:8.
2. Job 2:9.
3. Job 2:10; Job 1:21.

INVITATION 8: CREATING SPARKS
1. "Man's Static Jacket Sparks Alert," BBC News, September 16, 2005, news.bbc.co.uk/2/hi/asia-pacific/4252692.stm.

INVITATION 9: LYIN' EYES
1. They can happen on land as well, though not as commonly.
2. Genesis 3:4-5.
3. Genesis 3:6.

INVITATION 10: THE GOOD SHEPHERD
1. "What Are the Darwin Awards?," accessed January 24, 2003, https://darwinawards.com/rules/.

INVITATION 13: ONE IN A BILLION
1. Current World Population, Worldometer, accessed January 24, 2023, https://www.worldometers.info/world-population/.

INVITATION 14: DANCING IN THE DRYNESS
1. University of Haifa, "World's First 'Self-Watering' Desert Plant: Desert Rhubarb," *ScienceDaily*, July 5, 2009, https://www.sciencedaily.com/releases/2009/07/090701102904.htm.

INVITATION 18: HITCHHIKING THROUGH LIFE
1. Martin, "Hunga Tonga-Hunga Ha'apai Volcano (Tonga): Floating Pumice from Recent Eruption Spreads in Pacific," Volcano Discovery, December 22, 2021, https://www.volcanodiscovery.com/hunga-tonga-hunga-haapai/news/165170

/Hunga-Tonga-Hunga-Ha-apai-volcano-Tonga-floating-pumice-from-recent
-eruption-spreads-in-Pacific.html.
2. Alison Ballance, "Havre—The World's Largest Deep Ocean Volcanic Eruption,"
Radio New Zealand, June 14, 2018, https://www.rnz.co.nz/national/programmes
/ourchangingworld/audio/2018648947/havre-the-world-s-largest-deep-ocean
-volcanic-eruption.

INVITATION 24: THE LONG HAUL
1. A few species of albatross live in the Northern Hemisphere. For example, the
black-browed albatross (*Thalassarche melanophris*) in the North Atlantic; and
the black-footed albatross (*Diomedea nigripes*) in the North Pacific.

INVITATION 27: NARROW MINDS THINK ALIKE
1. Homer, *Iliad*, bk. 11, trans. A. T. Murray (New York: G. P. Putnam's Sons, 1924),
485.

INVITATION 29: WHY MATH?
1. *Peggy Sue Got Married* (1986), Twentieth Century Fox Home Entertainment,
written by Jerry Leichtling and Arlene Sarner. Directed by Francis Ford Coppola.
2. Eugene P. Wigner, "The Unreasonable Effectiveness of Mathematics in the
Natural Sciences," *Communications on Pure and Applied Mathematics* 13,
no. 1 (1960): 2.

INVITATION 34: HIGH AND MIGHTY
1. Miles O'Brien and Ann Kellan, "Dragonflies: The Flying Aces of the Insect
World," National Science Foundation, October 3, 2011, https://web.archive.org
/web/20170205195538/https://www.nsf.gov/news/special_reports/science_nation
/dragonfliesinmotion.jsp?WT.mc_id=USNSF_51.

INVITATION 38: BELOVED OUTCAST
1. Michael Guillen, "Michael Guillen: Why Is Pluto No Longer a Planet? The Answer
May Surprise You (Here's Why It Also Must Change)," Fox News, February 15,
2020; https://www.foxnews.com/opinion/pluto-no-longer-a-planet-michael
-guillen.

INVITATION 40: HUMAN FOLLY
1. The water must be at least 80°F.
2. Tropical depression (25–38 mph winds), tropical storm (39–73 mph), hurricane
(74+ mph).

INVITATION 41: ROOTS
1. Peter Wohlleben, *The Hidden Life of Trees: What They Feel, How They Communicate—
Discoveries from a Secret World*, trans. Jane Billinghurst (Vancouver, BC: Greystone
Books, 2016), 183.

2. Martin Luther King Jr., "The American Dream" (Sermon, Plymouth Church, Brooklyn Heights, New York, February 10, 1963).

INVITATION 42: DIVINE CREATIONS
1. Joni Mitchell, "Big Yellow Taxi," 1970, Siquomb Publishing Corp/BMI.
2. Genesis 1:2-3.

INVITATION 45: SIZE ISN'T EVERYTHING
1. "Penguin Chicks Rescued by Unlikely Hero," *Spy in the Snow*, BBC Earth, video, 3:46, accessed February 7, 2023, https://www.youtube.com/watch?v=IvkfpgjBt5k.

INVITATION 46: LIFE SUPPORT
1. Columbia University Medical Center, "Skeleton Is an Endocrine Organ, Crucial to Regulating Energy Metabolism," *ScienceDaily*, August 10, 2007, https://www.sciencedaily.com/releases/2007/08/070809130039.htm.

INVITATION 47: LIFE FORCE
1. Sarah DeWeerdt, "An Unlikely Wildlife Rebound in Chernobyl," *Anthropocene*, October 6, 2015, https://www.anthropocenemagazine.org/2015/10/chernobyl-has-become-an-unlikely-wildlife-haven/.
2. DeWeerdt, "Unlikely Wildlife Rebound."

INVITATION 57: A SLOW DEATH
1. Sigmund Freud, *Beyond the Pleasure Principle* (London: International Psycho Press, 1922), 47.
2. John 16:33.
3. John 11:25-26.

INVITATION 58: BY DESIGN
1. "Martin Rees—Why Cosmic Fine-Tuning Demands Explanation," *Closer To Truth*, YouTube video, 5:59, January 23, 2017, https://youtu.be/E0zdXj6fSGY?t=221.

INVITATION 62: LIKE A WEED
1. Ecclesiastes 2:10-11.

INVITATION 67: A CONSTANT IRRITATION
1. Susmita Baral, "World's Largest Natural Giant Clam Pearl Worth $130 Million Was Sitting Under a Fisherman's Bed for 10 Years," *International Business Times*, August 24, 2016, https://www.ibtimes.com/worlds-largest-natural-giant-clam-pearl-worth-130-million-was-sitting-under-2406471.
2. Rhonda Spencer-Hwang, *Raising Resilient Kids: 8 Principles for Bringing Up Healthy, Happy, Successful Children Who Can Overcome Obstacles and Thrive Despite Adversity* (Carol Stream, IL: Tyndale Refresh, 2021).
3. 2 Corinthians 12:7-9.

INVITATION 69: LIFE FROM DEATH

1. Chris Dart, "Fungi Are Responsible for Life on Land as We Know It," *The Nature of Things* (blog), CBC, January 24, 2023, https://www.cbc.ca/natureofthings /features/fungi-are-responsible-for-life-on-land-as-we-know-it.

INVITATION 70: A MYSTERIOUS LIGHT

1. *Einstein: A Centenary Volume,* ed. A. P. French (Cambridge, MA: Harvard University Press, 1979), 138.

INVITATION 71: COAT OF MANY COLORS

1. Ralph A. Lewin and Phillip T. Robinson, "The Greening of Polar Bears in Zoos," *Nature* 278, (March 29, 1979), 445–447, https://www.nature.com/articles /278445a0.

INVITATION 72: HEART TRANSPLANT

1. Morris Agaba et. al., "Giraffe Genome Sequence Reveals Clues to Its Unique Morphology and Physiology," *Nature Communications* 7, no. 11519 (May 17, 2016).

INVITATION 73: PROVIDENTIAL PROVISIONS

1. J. S. L. Edington, "White's Thrush: Some Aspects of Its Ecology and Feeding Behaviour," *South Australian Ornithologist* 29 (1983), 58, https://birdssa.asn.au /images/saopdfs/Volume29/1983V29P057.pdf.
2. Edington, "White's Thrush," 59.

INVITATION 80: FOLLOW THE LEADER

1. Zhi-Ming Yuan et al., "Wave-riding and Wave-passing by Ducklings in Formation Swimming," Cambridge Core, October 5, 2021, https://www.cambridge.org/core /journals/journal-of-fluid-mechanics/article/waveriding-and-wavepassing-by -ducklings-in-formation-swimming/94759A0FF7070D9D7CAC5907594B1781.

INVITATION 82: STELLAR CREATION

1. Kenneth G. Libbrecht, *Snow Crystals: A Case Study in Spontaneous Structure Formation* (Princeton, NJ: Princeton University Press, 2022).
2. "Snowflake Science," SnowCrystals.com, accessed January 23, 2023, http:// snowcrystals.com/science/science.html; see: "The Snow Crystal Morphology Diagram."
3. *The Journal of Henry David Thoreau, Volume 8, November 1855 to August 1856,* eds. Bradford Torrey and Francis H. Allen (Salt Lake City: Peregrine Smith Books, 1984), 87, www.doyletics.com/arj/tjr08rvw.shtml.

INVITATION 85: INITIAL CONDITIONS

1. Pierre-Simon Marquis de Laplace, *A Philosophical Essay on Probabilities*, trans. (from the 6th French ed.) F. W. Truscott and F. L. Emory (New York: John Wiley and Sons, 1902), 4.

INVITATION 88: THE VOICE
1. 1 Kings 19:12, KJV.

INVITATION 89: BLESS YOUR HEART
1. D'Arcy Power, *Masters of Medicine* (New York: Longmans, Green, 1898), 150–151.
2. Carmat 2018 Registration document, https://www.carmatsa.com/carmat-content /uploads/2019/03/carmat_ddr-2018_en_final.pdf.

INVITATION 91: UNQUENCHABLE LOVE
1. Kristján H. Kristjánsson, "Volcanic Eruption in Heimaey 1973," InterestingWorld .info, January 24, 2014, http://www.interestingworld.info/volcanic-eruption -heimaey-1973/.
2. Kristjánsson, "Volcanic Eruption."

INVITATION 93: HEALING FROM THE INSIDE OUT
1. Interview in 2005 of Dr. Byron Johnson, quoted in Jerry Newcombe, "Go to Church, Live Longer and Happier," *Christian Post*, January 16, 2020.

INVITATION 94: SHELTER FROM THE STORM
1. AccuWeather senior meteorologist Dan Kottlowski, quoted in Michael Kuhne, "What Is Tornado Alley?" Yahoo News, May 1, 2018, https://news.yahoo.com /tornado-alley-133327933.html.
2. "Safe Rooms," FEMA, accessed January 24, 2023, https://www.fema.gov/emergency -managers/risk-management/safe-rooms.

INVITATION 96: BEFORE YOU KNOW IT
1. *Merriam-Webster*, s.v. "peregrine (*adj.*)" accessed January 24, 2023, https://www .merriam-webster.com/dictionary/peregrine.

INVITATION 97: TRUE COLORS
1. Sir William Bragg, *The Universe of Light* (London: G. Bell and Sons, 1936), 1.

Topical Index

Scripture Index

About Dr. Michael Guillen

Michael Guillen was born in East Los Angeles, earned his BS from UCLA and his MS and 3D PhD from Cornell University in physics, mathematics, and astronomy. For eight years he was an award-winning physics instructor at Harvard University.

For fourteen years, he was the Emmy-award-winning science editor for ABC News, appearing regularly on *Good Morning America, 20/20, Nightline*, and *World News Tonight*. Dr. Guillen is the host of the History Channel series *Where Did It Come From?*; producer of the award-winning family movie *Little Red Wagon*; and host of the popular weekly podcast series *Science+God*, operated by K-LOVE and Air1 Radio.

Dr. Guillen has written op-eds for many, influential media outlets, including the *Wall Street Journal, U.S. News & World Report*, and Fox News.

He is a popular speaker worldwide and the bestselling author of *Bridges to Infinity: The Human Side of Mathematics*; *Five Equations That Changed the World: The Power and Poetry of Mathematics*; *Can a Smart Person Believe in God?*; *Amazing Truths: How Science and the Bible Agree*; *The Null Prophecy*; and *The End of Life As We Know It: Ominous News From the Frontiers of Science*. His newest book is *Believing Is Seeing: A Physicist Explains How Science Shattered His Atheism and Revealed the Necessity of Faith* (Tyndale Refresh, 2021), an Amazon #1 bestseller.

Dr. Guillen runs an all-media production company, Spectacular Science Productions, and is cofounder and principal partner of Accelarise Media.

For more information, see www.michaelguillen.com.

My Personal Journal of
Awe and Wonder

.....

**WHAT WONDERS DO YOU SEE IN THE WORLD?
MAKE NOTE OF THE WONDERS YOU SEE EVERY DAY.**

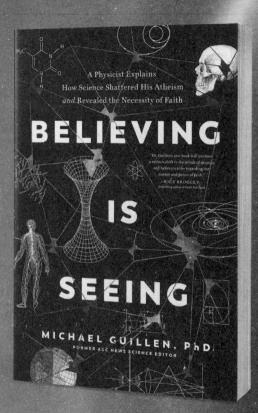